T0197184

SURRENDER YOURSELF

Dianne Crows

BALBOA.
PRESS
A DIVISION OF HAY HOUSE

Balboa Press books may be ordered through booksellers or by contacting:

Balboa Press
A Division of Hay House
1663 Liberty Drive
Bloomington, IN 47403
www.balboapress.com.au
1 (877) 407-4847

Print information available on the last page.

ISBN: 978-1-5043-0098-8 (sc)
ISBN: 978-1-5043-0099-5 (e)

Balboa Press rev. date: 01/18/2016

I would like to dedicate this book to;

My son Gavin
My daughter in law Sarina
My grandchildren Cody and Chloe
My niece Peta
My dearest friend Kathy
My good friends Jen and Jocelyn
My previous neighbour Carol
My good friend Donna, for assisting me with publishing my story
And to Donagh, for without her, this book
would not have been written

Learn from yesterday,

Live for today,

and

Hope for tomorrow

Albert Einstein

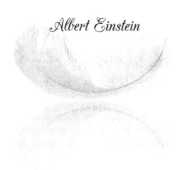

We all have our own beliefs, I guess.

I always knew there was more to life than to touch, see, and smell. I remember my mum going for psychic readings when I was in my teens. It fascinated me but she never spoke of anything she had been told by the psychic reader.

I was pregnant and married at eighteen and thought I had it all; we were travelling around Australia with all our belongings in a panel van. That was the seventies for you, not a care in the world.

We made it as far as Townsville when, the car broke down. It was the bell-housing, and we had no money to fix it. So John, my husband, got a job and we moved into a caravan park. My brother Dennis, his wife Glenda and her family were staying there too. We had company for a while, but they moved on and kept travelling. I remember spending most of my time cramped in the caravan.

I was glad when December arrived; it was time to have my baby. I had no idea what I was in for, or what to expect; I had no one to tell me. I was on my own with this one, and on December, 5, 1974, a nine pound baby boy was born. We named him, Gavin, and that little boy was what helped keep me strong for the next twenty years.

Six weeks after Gavin was born, we had the car up and running again and off we headed- unregistered, no driver's license, and with a baby in the back. We were headed to New South Wales and guess what? We made it all the way, not a cop to be seen.

Scone was our destination. Mum and Dad had bought a pub called the Willow Tree Hotel. Things were looking up. We had somewhere to stay, and I had a job, and a mum to help with the baby. I worked in the pub and John worked in a bike shop across the road from the pub for a while. We stayed in Scone for two years, and then moved to Aberdeen. When Mum and Dad sold the pub, I ended up with a job at the meat works. I stayed there for a few years, and Jon worked there as a fitter. I made a lot of friends there, including a few who were 'interesting' to say the least. Like the Knights, I'm sure some of you have read that story. My brother Dennis, moved to Scone after seeing them a few years earlier in Townsville, but sadly, by that time, he and Glenda had separated, and he was with his new partner, Pam. Dennis and Pam only stayed a few months. They headed back to Townsville where they stayed. After some time, Mum and Dad had packed up and moved to Orange. I missed Mum and Dad; we often went over for a weekend.

My marriage was a struggle from day one. I guess I just wanted things to work and Gav to have a father. Who the hell was I kidding? After we moved to Denman, I was working at the Royal Hotel as a barmaid and I hated it. Gav had started school for the first time at Martindale, a very tiny school, just out of Denman. I remember that look on his face that first day, God love him. John was working at a lawn mower place in Muswellbrook, but we didn't stay there long.

We moved back to Aberdeen and I went back to the meat works. John got himself a job working in a bike shop in Muswellbrook, so he was in his glory. It was a Harley Davidson shop and he came to own many Harley's. He loved buying the early model 65 pan

3

knuckle and shovel head motors that looked like they were ready for the scrap heap. He would rebuild them; he was very good at it, and always made good money when he sold them. With new cash in hand, he would head off to Mount Wilson to buy the next one. My lounge room often had bike parts in there getting rebuilt.

We had made good friends with the one family, Bev, Wes and Toni. Gav and their son, Toni, were at the same school, Aberdeen Public.

We learned that a house six miles out of town was up for rent, so we moved out there. The only thing wrong with that location was that we only had one car. Guess who had that car all the time? I used to walk home from work. Gav and I were stuck at home all weekend by ourselves; too bad if I needed milk or bread, but we entertained ourselves. I always thought Gav would be a fire fighter living out of town. We had a two hundred litre drum set up in the back yard to burn the rubbish, and every time you would look out the window, there was Gav lighting and stoking the fire. He was fascinated by it.

After we had lived there for a few years, I finally got my own car. It was a Volkswagen, and it was about time I had my own car! Most weekends, John was out with his mates, and he only came home for a shower and a feed before heading off to the next party. I was tired of being alone, so I made a decision; Gav and I would be better off on our own. I packed what I could in the car, and Gav and I, went off into the sunset on our own. We headed towards a town called Orange.

Mum and Dad lived in a block of units there, and Gav and I stayed with them for a while. I got a job at the Telford Motor Inn as a house maid, where I made myself a good friend. Gav got settled into Bletchington School. My sister Sharyn moved over with her four children, Kristy, Trevor, Peta and Megan. Gav and I loved that, and we were always together. Each child would take it in turns in sleeping over.

After a year or so, John and I had reconciled, and we moved back to Muswellbrook. John had rented a beautiful unit, and we set up again. I got a job at a local motor inn as a tray maid. Gav started high school and John was doing shut down work at a power station and bringing in good money. Once again I made some good friends, but when work started to die down for John, we had another decision to make.

By this time, Mum, Dad, Sharyn and her four children had all moved to Townsville, so we decided to give it a go. We packed up and headed back to Townsville to live back with the family again. We sold all our furniture and headed off on another adventure. After a long two-day drive, we made it. We moved in with the family until we got settled in with jobs and our own house.

On the second day, I ended up in hospital with a blood clot in my left calf. I remember going into a panic. Thirty years earlier, my pop had died of a blood clot, but my sister Sharyn reassured me I would be fine. Things had changed a hell of a lot, since Pop died, she reminded me, and that made me feel a whole lot better. On my third day in hospital, I had my first spiritual experience. I was just lying on the bed when a voice spoke to me.

"Have a look at your drip."

I was confused; I didn't know who said that. I looked down and noticed there was air in the tube leading to the cannula on my hand, so I pinched the drip at the end of the fluid. I'm not sure why I did that, but it seemed to be the right thing to do. I called for a nurse, and she sprang into 'panic station' mode immediately. The drip was pulled out, and replaced by a new one in the other hand. Great, I thought, another jab with a needle, I was already feeling like a pin cushion. When things settled down, I asked the nurse what had happened. I didn't understand why people were in such a panic. She explained that someone must have been watching over me that day, because if I haven't noticed the air bubble in time, it could have gone into my vein, and I would have had a massive heart attack. I don't know if I should thank my Pop, or an angel, but I am, sure that someone was looking out for me that day. I never mentioned it to anyone; no one would have believed me anyway.

John and I found jobs and a nice place to live. Gav was going to Pimlico State High School and things were good. I had my family with me and we did everything together. I loved being with my brother Dennis. On Friday nights we often had beers and homemade hamburgers. There were about fifteen of us, and these were the best nights with lots of laughs. We stayed there for a few years. I was working in a commercial laundry, running the wash room. I lost heaps of weight, as it was always sweaty. I hated the humidity, but I always made the best of things and made friends.

Once again, work was not looking good for John. John had gone to have a week with his mate in Swansea. I remember that week, as a cyclone was brewing. It ended up just being a lot of rain and high winds. While John was in Swansea, his boss rang to let John know that he would have to let him go. He suggested that if John could get work where he was, he should go for it. Once again, we packed up our lives. We moved back to New South Wales, where we moved in with John's mate Danny who owned his own house. We all got along so it was working out fine. Mum and Dad, by this time, had moved back to Orange, and Gav and I decided to head over for a few days. That was not good, Gav got offered an apprenticeship with my brother in-law as a painter and decorator and decided to stay. I knew he would be fine. Gav was living with Mum and Dad, and my little boy was growing up.

John was working in Sydney traveling back and forth every day and I was working in a laundry at Cardiff. Danny sold his house and we all rented a house together at Caves Beach. I went as often as I could to Orange to see Gav. I always travelled with my Aunty June, as it gave her a chance to be with her sister. We went by train and always had a good trip and some good laughs.

'I am'

and

'Gratitude'

Are the most powerful words

My dad was very sick. My dad had a lawn mower accident when I was in my teens. He was mowing the grounds near a heated swimming pool, and the blade had come off the mower, and had gone through his ankle. The blade was stuck in his ankle for hours, as they had to work out the best way to remove it. Maybe if they had taken his leg off at his knee, while he was still young, then perhaps, it would have made things a lot easier for him. My dad had nothing but trouble with his ankle and leg for the following twenty years. The doctors now decided to remove his leg off at the knee, which had made it very hard at his age and for Mum.

My sister was good and helped Mum and Dad a lot. Sadly my dad went back for another operation and died on May, 7, 1992. My mum was devastated; she had lost her soul mate. My sisters and I had lost our dad and the children had lost their pop. This was a sad time in my life, and I felt a piece of my heart was taken. I felt empty and I was glad that Gav was there to stay with Mum in her bad times. I knew he would be good company for her and would keep her busy.

John had realized how much I missed Gav and he also quite liked the town, Orange. So we packed up and moved back to Orange. I was glad we were back as a family again. I worked in the meat works at Blayney for a while, until I got a job in Orange at the Calare Nursing Home in the laundry. I made the most amazing friends and had the best laughs and good times with these guys, Denise, Sue, Margaret, Justin and Donna. I had lost track of them for a while, but thanks to Facebook, found them again. That's where I met Kathy, who is my dearest and best friend.

Living back in Orange was also good for Mum, as we could spend time together. Mum would always visit on Sunday, and would cook some scones and a few slices. I would cook a baked dinner, and then drop Mum back home. Gav was now working for the council and was starting to make some really good mates.

By the time I had reached my late thirties, I had the most amazing collection of American Indian things. Some I brought myself and a lot given to me as gifts. Even a tee-pee that actually smoked, that came from America. My home was full of American Indian stuff, but at the time never thought any more about it. But I guess, even then, someone was trying to get my attention. Being married to a non-believer of the spiritual world, I never read anything into it and life went on. In all the moves, I managed to give away all my American Indian things. All except this one Indian medicine bag, I had brought myself. I was attracted to this medicine bag and for some reason and hung onto it. You know what they say, everything happens for a reason. I am a firm believer that if you are meant to have a special gift, you will have it, and the universe will find a way to make it happen. I know what mine is now, but I didn't know at the time.

Seven years had passed quickly. I was in my forties, and my life was not good. My son, who kept me strong and gave me something to focus on, had suddenly grown up and found the love of his life. He had met Sarina who is a very kind, caring and loving girl. He had fallen in love with Sarina and they eventually married.

I had found myself with a Jack Russell pup. My husband brought me the pup for my birthday. This pup, Jack, stayed in my life for the next seven years filling the lonely void in my life. I dedicated my life to my pup, Jack. That way; I didn't have to focus on my marriage or its problems. I had a lot lessons to learn.

We were on the move again, only this time, I was going back to Townsville with no son. I'll always remember that drive. I was in my car, with a dog and a bird, and John was driving his car. I cried all the way, worried about what I had done, so I convinced myself, this will fix my marriage and all will be good.

We moved in with my brother, Dennis, and his family. I remember the date, as it was September, 11, 2001; the day of the devastation in America. We found a flat to rent and we were only in it for four months, until we finally brought our first house. I could see the potential, as it was an old Queenslander. I was back working in a laundry and John was working for a large franchise company. We had to drive back to Orange in February, for Gav and Sarina's wedding. We drove down and back in four days, John, Dennis, Pam and I. What a trip, but a beautiful wedding. Sarina was finally taking my place and taking care of my boy. You know that old saying 'A daughter always needs her mother, but a son chooses his wife.' But in saying that, we were blessed with this wonderful person.

Life went on and I was working long hours and spending time by myself. Until the day that Gav and Sarina headed up for a holiday with us, with Sasha, their dog. We called Sasha, Jack's brother, as Sasha and Jack spent every day together. I was beside myself watching every car coming around the corner. I was excited to show them this house we had brought and the potential, and seeing my son again. I had a great two weeks with them, but yes, it came to an end and they were heading back to Orange. I was again crying all day.

I came home from work one day to find John with a big smile on his face. John had said Gav had rung, and I have some good news. I started to get excited. John said "Settle down, no, they are not moving here." My heart sunk. John then said "But they are moving to Brisbane which was only one and a half hour's flight away." I thought "That's right, things weren't so bad." I walked around all night with a smile from ear to ear.

I got to spend every Sunday with my brother, Dennis. It was our time, and I loved it. I remember having a psychic reading with Pam Goodman, a few years earlier. Pam said, you don't know your brother on a heart level, but you will. I didn't understand what she meant at that time, but I do now.

My brother always headed out to the dump early Sunday morning, with a trailer full of palm leaves and rubbish. That was something he and his black bum staffe dog did together. He loved animals, just like I did.

Before I go any further with this, I had a dream about six weeks earlier. I dreamt that I had gone to look out our window from the high set house we lived in, and was looking down. In the dream, there was my brother, in his car slouched over his wheel. When I woke up, I thought to myself, what a strange dream. My brother loved his beer, big time, so I put it down to another drunk night.

It was about the middle of February, on a Sunday, when I got a phone call. My brother was on the way home from the dump, and had had a massive heart attack. Two army guys found him. He had crossed four lanes of traffic and ended up in front of a row of shops, slumped over his car wheel, with his dog licking his face trying to wake him up. It was very early and there was not much traffic around. Thank God or there could have been more people involved in a car crash. There was the dream.

I was a mess. I rushed to the hospital and found his family. You can imagine how they were, especially his children. The doctor finally came to meet with us saying it didn't look good. They didn't think he would make it. He had had a massive heart attack and had done major damage to his heart. He was in a coma with tubes attached to his body everywhere. This couldn't be my brother. He was fit and healthy and loved life. Things like this just don't happen to us, only other people. I bet everyone thinks like that. I prayed like never before. Please God, don't let my brother die. I have just connected with him again. I need him. He made life bearable. He couldn't die and leave me. Please, please, please. I waited for that phone to ring all night. It didn't ring, so there was hope, as he made it through the night.

For the following week, I was by his side. Mum had flown up as soon as I had rung and told her. I remember one night sitting with him by myself. A nurse had told us to keep talking to him. All the time, I was holding his hand, telling him about my day, when I said just out of the blue, I don't even know what made me say it. "Dennis are you OK, can you hear me?" "Is there something you want to tell me?" All of a sudden he leaned forward and said "Pam, Pam, Pam" in this horrible voice, and laid back down. He was in a coma and just scared the shit out of me. I was white and shaking, and I called for a nurse. He had just tried to speak. The nurse looked at him and checked out the machine. All was fine and then looked at me with that look, you know what I mean. What the hell, had just happened. Pam was his wife. When I got home, I still must have looked white. John asked how Dennis was and what was wrong. I told him what happened.

Dennis was in hospital for three weeks and a decision had been made to bring him out of his coma and see if he could breathe on his own. To our amazement, he pulled though and after a few days, his heart tracker was coming out. I was excited as my brother was coming back. I was beside myself. Every day after work, I would rush home, have a shower, and Mum and I, would head to the hospital. I never saw his wife Pam much. His wife never seemed to be there, as she always went late at night.

I remember this day well; Mum and I were sitting either side of Dennis' bed and were talking in general about when he got out, what we were going to do. Now you must remember this, my brother was straight down the line. He didn't believe in anything spiritual. That was all bullshit to him. But on this day, he looked at me and said "You know there is a tunnel." I replied "What?" He said "There is a tunnel of white light, but no one was there, so I didn't step in." I bet my eyes were like saucers and my ears pricked right up. I tried to calmly speak and said "Yeah, whatever!" "You don't have to worry about that." But trust me, I got into the car afterwards with Mum, and said, did you hear that, I knew it, I knew it.

I am me

Not you

Not he

Not she

But me

We were up to six weeks now. Dennis looked good, but had done massive damage to his heart. He was strong enough now to have open heart surgery. I was thinking that he would have a few more weeks in hospital and then come home. While I was hoping life was looking good again, things didn't go as planned. Dennis had another heart attack on the operating table and was now on life support machines, which were breathing for him.

My sister and some of the family flew up. My sister Sharyn and I had gone in to see him. The hospital visiting rules were only two at a time to visit. As we stood either side of his bed, he did it again; I squeezed his hand and said "Big Shazz is here." He then made a smile and said "mmmmm." Sharyn and I were amazed. It was as though he was happy and confirming that all the family was there finally with him. It was once again another mind blowing experience.

After a few days all the family had been called together for a meeting with the doctors. The doctors explained Dennis' condition and said he had one in a thousand chance of surviving. The machine was all that was keeping him alive. The doctors recommended we turn the machine off, and gave us until the next day to meet again.

I never slept that night. I felt sick all night and prayed. The next day we all were back at the hospital in the same meeting room. I could feel my heart thumping. How could I play God? As we sat around, in came two doctors. The doctors explained it all again. The doctors went around the room asking each family member, one by one, their decision. I could hardly see out of my eyes. Tears were dripping off my chin, as I heard each family member say "Yes." How could they do this? Then it was my turn. No way! My mum was with me on this one. But we were the only two. We were outnumbered. We all went back into Dennis' room and stayed with him until his last breath. The machines were turned off and unplugged. Within 20 minutes, he was gone and so was a part of me. I guess someone was there to meet him this time in the tunnel.

I thought it was bad for me, but what about Mum. She had lost her son; no parent should ever bury their child. Then there were Dennis' children grieving for their father and Pam had lost her husband. How were we ever going to get through this? I remember walking my dog, Jack, at 2am in the morning, angry and punching the air and saying how dare he, how dare he leave me here by myself with John. He had no right. If you're here, come hold my hand. I needed you and you left me. Now what was I going to do with my life. The things that were keeping me afloat in life were all slowly slipping away from me.

We started to fly down to Brisbane and visit Gav and Sarina. This was good, giving me something to focus on. When we came home, I was saving for the next trip to visit. The final turning point in my life was Christmas 2004. We drove down to Gav's home in Brisbane and headed over to my niece Peta's home in Kingaroy. It was a great Christmas and I had the best time. Peta and Ged always made you feel welcome.

I remember John was on their computer a lot, looking at houses, which I never thought much about at the time. As John and I were driving back to Townsville, John talked about the houses on the internet he had looked at. He had been doing some thinking about selling our home and buying a home closer to where Gav was. I thought, don't you dare put this thought into my head, it is not funny. But John said he was serious and had thought about it. John said that he could get a transfer with the large franchise business he was working for and I could find a job. So you can imagine what is going on in my head by now. We discussed it all the way home on the twelve hour drive and had it all worked out. My life felt good again and back on track. Back living near my son Gav.

To my surprise, John came home after his first day back at work and told me that he spoken to his boss about the transfer and said that would not be a problem. John just needed to let his boss know when he would like to do it. O MY GOD! This was really going to happen. During the next few weeks, we searched the internet for houses for sale. I was so excited to tell Gav we were moving down. I started packing up the house and John had spoken to the bank to get a bridging loan. Gav looked at a few houses for us, but in the back of my mind something kept saying, this is going way too smooth.

We ended up finding a perfect house for sale. Gav went and checked it out, then went back for a second viewing with Sarina. I knew if Sarina said it was good, it would be, as she liked to keep her own home perfect. I decided not to give notice at work until we had brought the house. Gav had rang his father and told him all about the house. It was perfect, so Gav organised for his dad to check it out on the coming Saturday. If the house was what we wanted, John was going to put a deposit on it.

The flight was booked and John was flying down at 7pm on Friday night. Gav would pick him up at airport Friday night and they would view the house on Saturday. John was going to phone me as soon as a decision was made about whether to purchase that house or not. I couldn't concentrate at work all week. I was so excited and was busting to tell someone, but kept it to myself. My current home was nearly all packed up and ready for a move.

Friday finally arrived. I had packed a bag for John. I just had to iron a pair of jeans when I got home from work. John's flight was at 7pm, so we needed to be at the airport by 6.15pm. Time was ticking away. It was 5pm and no John. Where was he? John finished work at 4pm and ended up strolling in at 5.30pm. Why did that not surprise me? You had better jump in the shower, we need to get going, I said. John said "Yep, you can iron my jeans." "All done" I replied. So I kept doing some more ironing while he had a shower and was just talking in general. When he got out of the shower and was getting dressed, he said as casual as ever "O'yeah, by the way, we are not moving to Brisbane." I said "What?" John replied "Yeah, no transfer, so were not moving." He never said another word, like it meant nothing. John still went to the airport and flew to Brisbane for the weekend. I was glad he went, as I cried all weekend. I didn't know how I would deal with it, or him, when he got back. I was so upset that I couldn't even phone Gav to tell him. I didn't think I could talk on the phone. As soon as John had left on the Sunday to fly back, Gav rang and asked what the hell was going on. Gav was upset to. Once again everything happens for a reason. I just didn't see it at the time. My heart was so broken. I felt my heart had been broken so many times; and felt at the time there was no way, it was ever going to mend.

My marriage was slipping away. I was sleeping in the front bedroom and John was in the spare room. I remember going to bed early one night and had another spiritual experience. I had shut the bedroom door and climbed into bed. There was a small gap under the door and you could see the light from the other rooms. As I rolled on my side, purple smoke started to come under the door and fill my bedroom. The purple smoke placed me in a very calm state. I looked up and there was a lady standing at the side of my bed and she said

"Look inside the cheese barrel."

I said "What?" and she repeated it again. "Look inside the cheese barrel." As I looked around my room, I realised it was full of dead people. I was still in a very calm state. Then as quick as it came, it went. I was thinking holly hell, what had just happened and who in their right mind would believe what had just happened to me. The next day, I checked my cheese tray in the fridge and checked all around and under the house. I also checked out my husbands' things, to see if he had anything that resembled a cheese barrel, but nothing. There has been nothing to this day to know what this meant.

I had unpacked most things and placed them back around the house. I left packed a few boxes of my personal items and stored them under my bed. I was feeling quite confused at this time. I was trying to sort this out in my head. I was trying to work out what I was going to do, and I needed something to focus on. That's when I got a phone call about something I had been waiting a long time for. It was late September 2005 and it was Gav. Gav had rung and as I answered he said "Mum, Are you sitting down?" I said "What is the matter?" "What has happened?" Gav then said those words, those precious words "We are having a baby." I was beside myself. O MY GOD! Finally, I was getting a grandchild. Then he asked "What would you like to be called." I said "Nan" "Please Nan." O MY GOD! A grandchild! I was over the moon. John, I'm not that sure of, as he had never been a father to his own son, let alone a grandchild.

Christmas 2005 was such a lonely Christmas, as we never went anywhere. However, early 2006 proved to be a turning point in my life. I was felt like I was finally getting my act together. I rang Gav one Sunday morning to tell him of an important decision. I was so nervous. As we spoke, I said "Gav, I'm leaving your father. I can't do this anymore." To my surprise, Gav said "Mum, you have to do what makes you happy." A felt like a weight had just been taken off my shoulders.

I was turning fifty in February 2006, and there was no way I was spending my 50th birthday alone with John. I wanted to be with my family and friends. I had made the travel arrangements. Firstly, I took a flight to Orange and had a few days with my friends from the nursing home. Denise picked me up at the airport, and I stayed with Denise and Jock. A party was arranged on the Saturday night with all my friends. We had the best night together. My side was sore from laughing all night. I had told them of my plans to leave John and they asked if I was serious. I told my friends, I was, and that I no longer wanted to make out that my marriage was good. It had been over for years, I just was not ready to face it. I certainly had some lessons to learn with more lessons to come. After a great time with my friends, I then needed to catch a train to my next destination.

I am grateful for all the lessons
That has made me a better
and stronger person

Jock took me to the train station on Wednesday to catch the train to Sydney. I then caught another train to Newcastle. Newcastle was where my sister and mum would pick me up and we would drive to a place called Wauchope.

It was February, 1, my birthday, the Big 50.

It was big; it was my turning point in life. Doesn't life begin at 50? Mine was about to.

The train trip was just what I needed, a very calm, relaxing time which gave me a chance to think about my life. As the train pulled in at the Cardiff station, there were two faces I knew and was looking forward to seeing, my mum and my sister. Mum looked good and our jaws never stopped on the drive to Wauchope, with a laugh or two.

Sharyn had a beautiful home with a pool, she was renting. Mum was living with Sharyn and her husband Trevor. We were having a party on the Saturday night for my 50th at Megan's place. John was flying down to Brisbane and driving down with Gav and Sarina. I had arranged a month before I travelled, for Sarina's family to come over. Sarina was thinking her family came for my party, but in actual fact, they were there for her baby shower. We arranged for the baby shower to take place on the Sunday. I had posted my things I had brought for the baby shower early, before I had left Townsville, so they would be there, when I arrived.

On the Thursday, it was a very hot day, so all of us girls ended up in the pool. I found this the best opportunity, as we were all floating around like beach whales, to tell them of my decision. I told them that I was leaving John and had made a decision to move to Brisbane and start a new life for myself. I did not know what reception I would get from them. I was ready to answer fifty questions, but once again my family all supported me. I asked if they could please not talk of it, as I had to talk to John myself, and tell him of my decision, and this weekend was not the time.

It was Saturday and everyone had arrived. It was awesome. Sharyn and her girls Megan Kristy and Peta had done a wonderful job along with all of the others who had helped with my party. The food was great and my cake was delicious. Right down to the decorations. I had even managed to get drunk with my sister on shots. It was a top night and Sharyn's girls were entertainers. They kept everyone laughing all night. A good night had by all.

There were a few hangovers on Sunday, after the party the night before. We had a great BBQ breakfast and after cleaning up, we set up for the baby shower. I had arranged with Gav to take Sarina out of our way during this time, so the baby shower would be a surprise. All went off well, Sarina had no idea. Sarina received some beautiful things for the baby. But mind you, Gav, Sarina, John and I, heading back to Brisbane in one car, our bags and baby gifts was a sight to see. Gav somehow managed to fit it all in. That was certainly one week to remember.

I loved my 50th birthday party, and loved all my gifts. Most of all I loved being with my family. It was excellent. There were some tears and off we headed to our destination of Brisbane. I still had another week with Gav and Sarina. John was heading back to Townsville the next day. Sarina and I dropped him off at the airport. Trust me, I wished I had been driving, I would of broke speed records to get him there and done a stop and drop, no let me rephrase that, a stop and throw. I had another week to get my head together.

I just love being with Gav and Sarina. I never wanted to go back to Townsville. Sarina gave me some very wise advice. Sarina said to me one afternoon sitting out on their back deck, with tears in my eyes "If you don't go home, it will never be over." "You need to face him and finish it."

Sarina was right once again. Here I was at the airport ready to go and face the music. It had to be done, and it had to be done the same day, as I arrived home, while I had the courage. I said my goodbyes and told Gav and Sarina, that I would see them in a month or two. I remember landing in Townsville and walking off the plane and heading down to pick up my bag and there stood John with a big smile. Nothing was ever wrong according to him. Life went on, so he dropped me at home and had to head back to work. John said he would see me again when he got home and then drove off. I felt sick, but was so happy to see my dog, Jack. I unpacked and did some washing, but my mind was going over and over what I was going to say when he got home. Then I heard the Ute drive in that afternoon. My heart was thumping; he had done what he always does, straight to the fridge for something to eat or drink, and then headed out in the yard with Jack.

I kept saying it has to be done. So with sweetie palms, off I headed down the stairs. John, I said "I need to speak to you." So we headed under the house and sat at the table and chairs and without hesitation I blurted it out. "It's over, I'm moving out." He had a surprised look on his face and replied "What are you going to do, get a flat?" I said "No way." "I'm moving to Brisbane." He said "I'm not following you there; get that out of your head." I replied with "It was over, did you not hear me! It's over, you and me, it is over…." We argued for quite a while that afternoon. I went to bed that night for the first time in a lot of years feeling relieved. As I started to tell my friends, I realised I was doing the right thing. The hardest thing of all was sitting my little Jack Russell on my lap, and trying to explain to him with tears dripping down my cheek, there was no way I could take him with me. John had loved this dog, the way I did, so I knew he would be taken good care of him, the way I did.

I rang Gav and told him it was finally over and would see him soon. I started packing and making plans and got a transport company to take my boxes. Gav picked them up at his end. I had given notice at work. John and I had settled our finances, as I just wanted out.

It was April 2006, a Monday night and what I had left, I fitted in my little red Hyundai. I spent my last night with Jack and set the alarm for 4.30am. I got up and showered. I had made some sandwiches, the night before. This was it. I kissed my little dog goodbye. I told him, I loved him, and would see him again one day. I put my budgie on the front seat and headed off for Brisbane. I had felt like this weight, that had been on my shoulders for years, had finally been taken away, as I drove down the road.

The first few hours it had rained and those who know me know that I hate driving in the rain and at night. I had planned to drive as far as I could and stay the night, then head off the next morning. My trip was fine only stopping for fuel, water and a bag of potato chips.

There was one fuel stop around one o'clock. I had a park at the side of it. Sam, the budgie and I perched up at a picnic table to have lunch. I had lamb sandwiches which I had made the night before. They were delicious and did the job. Sam nibbled on the crust, then off we headed. Poor Sam was hanging on his perch for grim death; as the cage bounced around all the way, God bless him.

By 5.30pm I had made it to Gympie and was excited. I rang Gav as I knew I was about two and a half hours drive from his place. I said "How are you, my love?" Gav replied "Good Mum, how are you going?" I then said "I'm traveling well; I have had an excellent run so far." "What are you having for tea?" Gav replied "Pasta." I then said "Well save some tea for me as I should be there by eight." "Shit" was his reply. "You are going well." With that I hung up, filled up with fuel for the last time, and headed off.

It was getting dark and I was getting tired, but getting closer. Driving down to visit in earlier times had made it easy for me to know which direction I was heading, as I approached Brisbane. There it was, the last set of lights with a sign saying Fredrick Street, which was my turn. Thank you God! I had made it safe and sound. While waiting for the lights to change, I rang Gav and said, open the gates. I arrived at 7.45pm, which was fifteen hours after leaving Townsville. I was absolutely buggered. I think I fell out of the car, but can't explain what it was like to see both of their faces. We grabbed Sam and left the car till the next day to unpack. We headed upstairs and had tea along with a shower which was well appreciated. I still could not believe I had done it. I didn't sleep well that night, as I had a lot going on in my head. Gav had the next day off work. We unpacked the car and stored some of the things. The rest went up to the spare bedroom.

Gav was excited to show me this house they were interested in buying. We went and checked it out. It was quite a nice place. Afterwards we needed to go to the vehicle registration office. While we were sitting there waiting for our number to be called, Gav and I talked about the house. I asked if it was what he wanted and whether he was sure this is the right house. Gav said "Yes Mum, we both love it." I then replied "Well make an offer on the house, but not at the price. If they won't come down in the price, you may have something in the middle to bargain with." He looked at me, then opened his phone and rang and made an offer. Now it was just a waiting game. Gav was excited. Our number was called out at the vehicle registration office and we did what we had to do, then left. Heading back to the car, Gav's phone rang; he looked at his phone and said it was the real estate phoning back. I left him to talk in private and kept walking to the car. As I turned around, there was no need to speak, his face said it all. Gav said "They accepted it Mum, they accepted." We were both excited at the news.

Some people are old at 18

And some are young at 90

Time is a concept that

humans created

Yoko Ono

As we drove off, I will always remember that look of excitement on Gav's face. We headed for Springwood. Sarina was working in a retail shop in the plaza and we were going to have lunch with her and fill her in on the good news. They were going to be proud owners of a new home.

Gav thought however, he would have a bit of fun first, and tell her they missed out. I saw the look of disappointment on her face, but it soon changed, when he told the truth. They were like two Cheshire cats, with smiles from ear to ear. Life was good. So their next couple of weeks was consumed with papers, real estate and the bank and all the things that go with buying a house. For me it was about getting a job.

Another rock in my life was my niece Peta. Even before I had left Townsville, Peta had asked me to send my Resume to her and she would update it. It was Easter and Peta and her children, Tee-arna and Jack were coming over to catch up and bring my Resume. I was so looking forward to a couple of days with them. The Resume she put together for me was unbelievable. We had a great time together, over the Easter long weekend and I told her, I would head to Kingaroy, as soon as I got myself settled.

I was on a mission to get a job. I went down to the closest shopping plaza and handed out about fifteen Resumes to different shops in the plaza. It didn't matter what kind of job, as long as it paid the bills. I also applied for a few positions over the phone. Straight across the road from Gav and Sarina was a nursing home. I strolled down their driveway Easter Sunday. Their reception was closed, but I remember hanging over the counter and placing a corner of my Resume under their computer. I was hoping on their return to work, it would stick out and they would not miss it. I remember when John and I used to visit Gav and Sarina; I thought it was a boarding school. Gav told me "No Mum, it's a nursing home." I remember standing at the gate, looking down the drive way, saying to myself, I'm going to work there one day.

It had been three weeks since I first started looking for work and I was beginning to worry. I needed a job now. Gav and Sarina were getting ready to pack to move to their new home. Sarina was also starting to get bigger due to her pregnancy and looking more tired.

I finally got lucky and accepted a position in a nursing home at Mount Gravatt. The position was working in their laundry. So on the weekend before commencing, Gav and I went for a drive to see how to get there. On the Monday morning, I left early to get a head start on traffic, as things on the roads were a lot different in Brisbane than Townsville. After a nervous start, I found my way. My first day went well. It would just take me a week to settle into the way they washed and folded. A lot different to a commercial laundry, trust me.

It was my rostered day off work on the Thursday. Sarina was off work too. We both headed down to do some shopping. As we were driving home, my phone rang. The lady phoning said "Is this Dianne?" "Speaking" I replied. The lady then said "Hi, I'm Alison" "We were wondering if you could come in for an interview tomorrow at noon." I was thinking who were they, and where were they located, and did I put a Resume in with them? I asked where they were located.

She said "Fredrick Street." I then thought, O MY GOD! That's the nursing home across the road from Gav. I told her that I was so sorry I would not be able to get there before 12.45pm. She said "That will be fine, I look forward to meeting you tomorrow" and hung up.

I must of had a disbelieve look on my face. Sarina said "Mum, What is wrong?" I replied "I just got an interview across the road at the nursing home." Sarina said "Mum, that's excellent." I was beside myself. I had to work tomorrow and I finished at noon. That gave me thirty minutes to get home, fifteen minutes for a shower and get down their driveway. I can do it. I just prayed the freeway was running, with no hold ups. All went to plan. I had clothes out ready to go. Then off I went down their driveway.

I arrived and was greeted by the lady at the front reception. I said "Hi, I'm here for an interview with Alison." The receptionist said "Dianne is it?" "Yes", I replied. The receptionist told me that she would let Alison know that I was here. Although, my hands were sweating, I always managed to hold it together in an interview.

I was asked to come in and was greeted by two ladies. One lady said "Hi Dianne, I'm Alison and this is our General Manager, Lynda." I reached out and shook their hands. The interview began and all went well. At the end, Lynda said, "We usually like to start new employees on a casual basis for a few months, and then make a decision, but I'm going to break the rules and offer you a permanent part time job in the laundry starting Monday." "I must say your Resume really stuck out and grabbed our attention." I was so grateful to Peta for such an awesome Resume. I shook hands and accepted the wage.

It was a bit less, but there were no tolls and petrol and better than travelling to the other job.

I rang the other nursing home, apologised, and explained I would not be back. I explained that I had been offered a job closer to home. All was good. I was very excited and couldn't wait for Gav and Sarina to arrive home and fill them in on my interview and my new job.

Both Saturday and Sunday were very busy. We were all moving to their new home and Sarina was under strict instructions not to go into labour. It was Saturday May, 13, 2006, and Sarina was due to have her baby any day. All weekend, we were back and forth moving loads of boxes. Sarina stayed at the new house unpacking what she could. We were all so tired by the Sunday night.

On the Monday, it was time to start my new job. I was so pleased with working so close to home. My job started fine and I was settling in. Gail was my offsider, and to this day we are good friends.

Soon after, my car arrived. It was a 1957 Chev 4-door pilarless. That was part of my settlement with my ex-husband, John. Gav thought I would be better off selling the Chev, and he would build a hot rod. He was the one doing all the work, and we could both make some money on it. So that's what we did. Gav had his fathers' gift. Johns' was bikes and Gavs' was hot rods. The Chev needed to have a few minor things done, before I could sell it. That would give Gav something to do while we were waiting on the arrival of their first baby.

I remember this day well. We were at a large hardware and gardening store on a Saturday, looking at some gardening items, when Sarina said "O' I think it is finally time." Gav was still looking around and thought she had been joking. I said 'Gav, we have a baby here ready to make an entrance'. Gav then replied "Oh, OK we'd better get out of here and go and get the bags and head to the hospital." I said "You think so." Sarina and I had a good laugh.

I was excited, as I had been asked to go in and watch my grandchild come into the world. It was about 7pm and Sarina was very uncomfortable with pain. The nurses kept checking contractions, but after a while, there seemed to be a complication. The baby had just turned around and headed back up as if to say, I'm not coming out there!!! So a decision was made. Sarina was rushed off and prepared for a C-section. I hoped this was going to be OK and I asked the angels to go in with her. I wasn't allowed in the theatre. Gav was taken in to be gowned up, to be present in the operating room. For now it was just a waiting game. Every time the theatre doors flung open, I was up on my feet in anticipation.

At 11.04pm on May, 27, 2006, the door flung open again. This time, it was my son holding this little bundle in his arms. I said "O MY GOD! Sarina!" Gav replied "She is fine Mum, we have a son." As my eyes meet my little grandson for the first time, I felt a piece of my heart would mend with this precious little soul. I looked at Gav and in the same breath; we both said it "An old man." Then Gav said it again "He looks like an old man." I said, "No Gav, he is an old soul." Trust me to this day, he is an old soul.

There was no sleep that night. There were people to ring and just a buss of high energy flowing around us. Sarina's mum and sister were heading up to Brisbane from Orange, as quickly as they could. Sunday was full of visitors coming and going with beautiful gifts and flowers.

It was perfect when Sarina's mum arrived. Although Sarina is like my daughter, it's nothing to the bond of her own mother. Some alone time with her mum and sister was just what Sarina had needed. I went back to the hospital on Monday night and there was a good mate of Gav's, Craig and his wife Donna and Samuel, their son. I had met them in earlier times. We would go out and visit them. I had felt a connection with Donna, but had no idea what would form between us later. The universe has a way of bringing people together and their son Samuel was born only two months earlier before Cody. That was my new grandson's name, welcome Cody Albert.

Sarina headed home from hospital with her precious cargo. I was living there, along with Sarina's mum and sister and their grandson Jordie also staying. With a full house, I felt like moving out in the shed to get out of the way at times.

Over the following few months, my work continued to be going great. Gav sold my 1957 Chev, which I got from my settlement with my ex-husband John. Gav was then on a mission to build a hot rod which would keep him busy for the next few years. I had also been over to Peta's and Ged's for a weekend and loved visiting them.

Just believe, believe, believe!

It was now August 2006 and Cody was three months old. I knew I needed my own space and to stand on my own two feet. I had been living with Gav and Sarina for long enough. I knew they needed their own space too. My life had been so full on since I moved to Brisbane, that I never had time to stop and see how I felt nor had I dealt with any of my issues. I needed to find out who I was and what I wanted out of life. I was craving a spiritual journey.

It was time for me, to find a place of my own. I needed to take stock of my life and what had taken place over the last twelve years. So after work I would go for a drive and looked around to see if I could find somewhere to live. On the third day of looking, I headed in the other direction. I turned left out of the drive way from work, and drove to the end of the street, and turned left into Short Street. As I drove down Short Street, just on the bend, I saw this big block of units. So I pulled up, looked in and drove off. I found myself heading back again the following afternoon to have another look. This time I parked in the car park and walked up to the gates and looked in. There was a pool area with a BBQ and palm trees. It looked beautiful, and the grounds were well taken care of with a bonus locked security gate. I thought I could see myself living there. I ended up writing down the number to ring. Despite my first attempt at ringing, the phone number ended up, not being correct. So I drove back down the next afternoon. There was a small access gate beside the main front gate. To open the small access gate, it appeared you needed a key. All the unit numbers were on the wall. By punching in the number of the unit, the person in the unit could answer their home and could open the gate. The security was an attractive bonus. I rang a number hoping that I could speak to someone. The lady who answered said "Hello can I help you?" I replied "Yes, I was wondering who I could speak to about a unit?" She responded with "Yes, by all means, that is me." "I will open the gate for you. Thank you."

I was excited. As I strolled in, she introduced herself. "Hi, I'm Judy." I replied "Hi, I'm Dianne." She said "Come on into the office." We sat for a while and I told her my story of where I was working. I told her that I was living with my son and daughter-in- law, and that I had been there way too long. She asked if I would like a villa or two storey unit. I said "I would love a villa please." She replied "Well I have two coming up, one in four weeks and one in six weeks." She couldn't show me inside a villa, as people were still living in them. Instead, she showed me the floor plan of the units and the design of the ones coming available. They were design two and three. The three bedrooms and ensuite looked great. Judy took some details and said she would check back in about two weeks. I thanked Judy for her time. I was excited to tell Gav and Sarina I had found myself somewhere to live. It was only two minutes to work. However, when I mentioned it to Gav, Gav said "Why do you want to live there?" "It's not a good area". But I said "Nope, I'm doing this."

I thought, now I needed a psychic reading to put the icing on the cake. I thought the psychic reader would say that I would meet a new man, have plenty of money and live happily ever after. There was a crystal shop in the nearest shopping plaza. I thought this is just what I needed, so I headed off. All will be good. After only thirty minutes wait, browsing the surrounding shops, the psychic reader was ready to see me. The psychic reader said "Hi, I'm Toni Owl-feather, come on in Dianne." I sat down in the little room all excited. He started talking mostly of my past. He then proceeded to tell me that I had a hell of a lot of healing to do before I could move forward with my life. He said that I needed to learn to love myself. He said that meditation would be perfect for me and knew the perfect group and the lady that ran it. He wrote down her phone number. He prattled on for another twenty minutes or so. I was not interested in what he was saying, as I had not yet heard, what I wanted to hear. I was thinking, how dare he, who does he think he is, he knows nothing about me. He handed me the phone number of the lady who ran the meditation group, and then I left. I was pissed off not hearing what I wanted to hear. However, for some reason, I kept the phone number of the lady who ran the mediation group.

I started to pick some furniture ready for my unit. Some bits and pieces for my lounge room were on back order, and would take a few weeks to come in. It was a Friday afternoon, two weeks after that miserable psychic reading. I had just come across that phone number I had been given. I thought I'm going to phone and go to meditation. Nothing ventured, nothing gained. Isn't that what they say? So I rang "Hi, I'm Dianne." "Toni Owl Feather gave me your number for meditation." She said "Yes, it's on tonight." "I'm Rayleen and its starts at 7pm." "You are most welcome." Rayleen gave me her address. To my surprise, it was just around the corner from Gav's home. At 6.45pm, I decided that I was not going. I thought I didn't need that shit with a bunch of strangers. No way! So I decided to concentrate on my unit instead.

Two more weeks had passed and I was excited about seeing an available unit. I called back in after work and Judy said that an old man in unit thirteen had moved out. The old man who used to live there was not well and needed to go into a nursing home. Judy told me that they were cleaning and putting new carpet in the unit. The unit would be ready to move into in a weeks' time. I paid my bond of two weeks rent and arranged for the electricity to be connected. That following Saturday, I signed my lease, ready to move in on September, 23, 2006.

The week leading up to moving in, I organised a few things for the unit. I was excited about moving in. On the Saturday morning of the move, I was up at six o'clock ready to start. My car was packed. Gav was bringing the larger furniture in the truck. I headed off. I had my gate remote and keys to the unit. I pushed the button on my remote and the gate opened. Gav was following behind me in the truck. I drove passed the pool and turned right down to unit thirteen. I said to myself "Sam the budgie and little red car, this is our new home." I opened the door and Gav and I headed in. It was a lovely looking unit. Even Gav said it was really spacious and lovely. The only downfall was a little court yard out the back, along with a tiny kitchen. But, it was only me, so it would be fine.

I unpacked my car and helped unpack the truck. Gav assembled my bed and set up the TV. We worked hard all day unpacking boxes and setting up the unit. That afternoon Sarina and Cody came around for a takeaway tea.

My first night took me quite a while to get to sleep all by myself. I was in a unit with some strange sounds to get used to. Waking up on Sunday morning was exciting. It was great having breakfast in my new unit on the first morning. The rest of the day was unpacking then I went and got some groceries.

A week had gone by and I was still waiting on my lounge to be delivered. I was sitting in camp chairs as they said another two weeks. I was not happy about the wait. My unit was all organised and things had come to a holt. I was all of a sudden lonely. I was fine while I was at work, which kept me busy. However, on the weekend, O MY GOD! what had I done! I found myself sitting in a camp chair looking around and up the hallway at the front door. Please someone ring me or come visit me. I'm so lonely, what am I going to do? How will I cope? Peta and I spoke once a week on the phone. Mum and I took it in turns, week about, ringing each and other. I also got to talk to my sister, as Mum was living with her. I looked forward to those phone calls.

I had been in my unit now for three weeks. I came across the phone number again for meditation group. I thought about it all day, I rang again, apologised, and asked would it be possible to come. As I pulled up in front of the house, my nerves were making me feel sick. I just don't do these sorts of things. I was worried about a house full of strangers. I kept on saying to myself "Breathe, Breathe, Breathe." I headed up the driveway as there was no turning back now. I was greeted with two big friendly dogs and a lovely lady who said "Hello, come on in." Everyone was sitting around the dining table and introduced themselves one by one. "Hi I'm Kylie." "I'm Sarita."

"I'm Gary and this is my wife Dorinda." and "I'm Rayleen." "Hi everyone, I'm Dianne." I told them that I was nervous and that I had never done this before. Everyone told me that I would be fine and would love it. After a while we headed to the lounge and settled in. Everyone had their own spot. Rayleen explained there was no right or wrong way to do it. Just go with the flow and listen to her voice and relax. It was an amazing night. We talked as a group afterwards and I felt that no one judged me.

The following morning, Sarina picked me up in her car. We were going to the markets and her first question was "Mum how was the mediation group?" I replied "O MY GOD! Sarina, I loved it." Those five people were amazing. We were both crying, as Sarina drove down the road. Sarina said "I'm so happy for you." The normal me would have never gone back to meditation group. But I loved this so much that I couldn't wait for the next fortnight to go again. Each time I went, it got easier and more comfortable. After meditation we would sit for hours talking at the table. I was learning so much on a spiritual level. I was amazed at the places I would go and the people I would see in my meditation. I went back down to the shopping plaza and personally hugged Toni Owl Feather, for what he had done, and how it changed my life.

I would often head over to Peta's place on my off weekend of meditation and she would come and stay with me when she could. Peta's place was so relaxing and nothing is a bother to Peta. Peta is an Earth Angel. A very kind and caring soul, who will go that extra mile to help whoever she could, no questions asked, and nothing in return. No wonder Mum loved it there. Peta would often drive down and pick up Mum. They would call in, and stay for a few days, and then head off. Mum went and stayed with Peta and her family for a month or two. That became a regular event and Mum loved it as much as Peta did.

I am grateful for the love
of family and friends
That, I am

I was still lonely when I was on my own. I could never do much, as I didn't have the money from one pay to the next. But my bills were paid and my fridge was full of food. I always looked on the bright side. I had a unit, a job, and a beautiful family. I also had a gorgeous grandson who I loved looking after on my days off, as Sarina went back to work a couple of days a week. Rayleen had given me a copy of 'The Secret' DVD and I was blown away by that. It started to change my way of thinking. I found the more books I read relating to this topic, the more grateful, I became.

Over the following few years, I had a number of spiritual experiences. But let me tell you, this beautiful unit had an evil side to it, and I was starting to find that out. The hallway had a terrible energy about it, walking up to my bedroom, which was at the front of the unit. I always felt like someone was there and following me. I would never walk around in the dark. I always turned on the lights. Things really started to get bad at night. I would get woken up with an ice cold finger on my lips, or someone jumping on my bed or pulling my hair. I would also get woken up by someone pushing on my back or even lying beside me. I would often hear them running up my hall into my bedroom. I would become so cold like ice. I always knew when they were there. I was so petrified that I couldn't even speak. I was that scared. I knew when they had gone, as I would warm back up. Who in their right mind would believe me? I would try to say "What do you want?" But could never get it out. I had been so scared. It was just a stutter. I hated it, and was glad to see the morning. By the morning, I was not sure, if it was just my imagination. That these things never happened. Or was it that I was just stepping on the spiritual side of life. I didn't know. Maybe it will just go away if I try and forget it.

My mum had come to stay again for a few days before heading to Peta's place. We spent a lot of our time out in the back courtyard of the unit and would talk for hours. I remember my mum asked one day "What's that lady, like across from you in unit five, she seems lovely." The lady living in unit five would sit out the front of her unit having a cuppa. I told Mum that I was not getting involved, as I didn't want people living on my door step.

A few days after Mum had left, and I had come home from work. There was a knock on the front door. My neighbor was standing there with a plate of cake. She said "Hi I'm Carol." "I just thought I would come an introduce myself." I replied "Hi, I'm Dianne." "Come on in, I'll put the jug on." There were a few moments of silence, but then the conversation would pick up again. As we said goodbye and I thanked her for the lovely cake. I shut the door and thanked God that I wouldn't be going there again! But over a few more conversations and cuppas, our friendship grew. Carol became one of my very good friends. We were good for each other. Carol's quiet side and my loud and wild side made us good friends for years. There were many days of swimming and then back on the veranda for port and chips. We had a good laugh. We were good bouncing blocks for one another and Carol showed me so many places around Brisbane. We had a lot of good times, without having to spend much money.

I remember Carol was heading overseas for six weeks. I thought how would I survive without her? But I did survive. It was another learning curve for me. Over time, Carol had a few more overseas trips and even found a partner, Terry. Life then changed again for me. I learnt to not lean on other people so much and to love myself even more. A good thing was we would catch up once a week, and still have our laughs. Carol was always there, if I needed something.

I was looking forward to my first Christmas with Gav, Sarina and Cody. We had it at Gav's and Sarina's home. It was wonderful. Our lunch was perfect. They had a few friends around and we had a great day with some good laughs. The little man got spoilt. Cody loved ripping the paper off the gifts. I brought him a little red wagon which he still has to this day. I got spoilt myself by Gav and Sarina. My favourite was a statue of an angel. The angel came up to my waist. I loved it. It was a wonderful Christmas day with my family, and a wonderful end to the year.

January 2007 was a start to a new year with good news. I was getting another grandchild. I was hoping for a girl that would complete their family. Regardless of whether it was a boy or girl, it didn't matter. As long as the baby was healthy and Sarina was fine.

My job was going well. I was the Supervisor of the laundry now and Gail and I had cleaned and organised it, so it functioned better.

I found myself slipping back to collecting American Indian items again. I was not sure why I was fascinated by them. I had found some beautiful dream catchers, and I had started to collect a variety of feathers.

Mum was still calling in from time to time and I would head to Peta's home when I could. I remember my friend Carol coming

over to ask would I like to go with her to the local RSL on Saturday
night. There was a band there and we could go boogie. I thought that
sounded excellent. I had not been out to dance, since I don't know
when. Here it was, Saturday night and I was excited. I got ready. I
went back and forth to the bathroom to check. I looked good and I
thought to myself, I can do this. As we headed off with Carol driving,
I remember starting to have a panic attack. Breathe, Breathe, Breathe!
We arrived and Carol signed me in. I thought; see I knew I can do
this. I got ourselves a drink and sat down. The music was good and
the place was buzzing. We were there for about two hours when all
of a sudden I looked around at all these men drinking, and went into
panic mode again. I don't want this. I don't want a drunk. I just want
to get out of here. I spoke to Carol and we left.

I really had some major work to do on that issue with men. I don't
know why I was thinking of a man. I had so much work to do on
myself, let alone think of a partner. I didn't want to attract the same
type of man back into my life again. I think that's the mistake a
lot of people make. Not allowing enough time to heal and going
straight back into another relationship and then bang, you end up
back where you started, experiencing the same relationship as the last
one. I have learnt that we need to take a step back and take a look
at what went wrong. What we need to change in ourselves, to make
ourselves a better person. To make a relationship work, it's give and
take from both sides, not just one.

My sister, Sharyn, Kristy, Peta and my good friend Kathy were
heading up for a week. I was excited, about a week of company and
my unit full of people. I had even arranged for a psychic reader on

the Friday to come to the unit. I had the best week and we never stopped laughing. We had gone shopping a few days and on the Thursday decided to go to some second hand shops. I had got some bargains from our shopping. While I was fossicking around, I looked up on the wall. There was a beautiful painting and thought I may have brought it. That's when something or someone kept saying "Hello, look down here." At my feet was the most amazing picture of an American Indian. The picture took my breath away. I couldn't buy this picture quick enough and get it home. I dusted it off and Kathy darkened the frame for me. I placed it in the lounge room where I could look at him all the time. I was in love with this picture, but I didn't know why. I had no idea who the man in the picture was.

After my visitors headed home, I was feeling lonely again. The unit felt empty. But I always managed to stop feeling sorry for myself and get on with things. That was my strong side.

Rayleen was selling a beautiful glass cabinet. The cabinet was the old type, where the two glass doors opened at the front and the shelves were also glass. The back of the cabinet was a mirror. It was beautiful. I brought it and it became my display unit for my feathers and some crystals. It looked amazing with my Indian pictures above it. Rayleen had also given me these two magnificent Indian figurines, which took place on the top of this cabinet.

Sarina's mum, Sue came to stay with Gav and Sarina, during August 2007. The new baby was due to be born and Sarina was a lot bigger with her pregnancy this time around. I was sure it was a girl. Sue was staying for a few weeks after the baby was born to help Sarina settle in with her two children. Cody was only fifteen months and just walking. Sarina would have her hands full.

I had Mum staying with me and we were all off to the hospital. It was Friday August, 24, 2007, and Sarina had been booked in for a C-section. It was another exciting day. Gav and Sarina had gone to get ready and we were in the waiting room like a bunch of hobos. We had our bags of crocheting, knitting and Cody's toys. You would have thought we were moving in for a month. Cody kept us busy, as he was into everything. Time seemed to move fast. Every time those doors flung open, we were watching. After a while, Gav came through the doors with no baby and his face was white. As I got to my feet and rushed to Gav, he said "O' Mum, what has happened, there was blood everywhere." I asked "What happened?" "Is Sarina OK?" Gav wasn't making much sense. Apparently, Sarina could feel them cutting her and she was bleeding badly. Gav was pushed out the door of the operating theatre, fast, so the doctors could do what was needed. But not long after Gav was called back in. We waited patiently and then Gav returned with this most precious little bundle in his arms. A baby girl! They got their girl, welcome, Chloe Rose. Sarina was OK, but very drained. By the time we got to see Sarina, she was sore and still drugged. Sarina needed some well earnt rest. Our new little girl was breathtaking and perfect in every way. This little girl is a free spirit in every sense of the word. I love my grandchildren. I thank God and the universe every day for these precious gifts.

I am grateful for the love and
support of my Indians
That, I am

I enjoyed going to my meditation group. I loved being with these beautiful people. I never stopped asking questions and learning more about the spiritual side of life. I also started dreaming a lot. Sometimes, I wondered where the dreams came from, as some of the dreams were not making sense.

I remember climbing into bed one night and just getting settled in, when I heard someone speak and say

"Tell them to go to the back of the bus."

I knew exactly what I had heard, and sat up all excited and clapped my hands. Yes, someone had just spoken, and I heard it. Not that it made any sense.

My visitors were still coming into my bedroom. Not all the time, maybe every couple of months. Most of the time I was still that scared person frozen, not being able to deal with it.

On weekends, I spent a lot of time sitting out in the back courtyard, just thinking and not realizing that I was healing myself. One day, I even got lucky, and saw an owl sitting in a small tree near the courtyard. From a spiritual perspective, that's a good thing to see. I was happy to see the owl as I knew I was on the right path.

It was the start of another year. I made it through the last year and felt a bit stronger. But I still didn't love myself. So 2008 was another year of healing.

I loved having the family over in summer, as we would head up to the pool. It was excellent to go to the pool in the unit complex where I lived. I taught my grandchildren how to swim and to love the water. Work was going fine, but after a hot day in the laundry at work, it was great to be able to come home and have a dip in the pool.

During a bush walk one day, I came across a good strong piece of broken branch on the ground. I picked it up. From the ground up, it came to my chest and was very straight. I had a vision to make something with it, so I brought it home. With black swede bound around it, feathers, and bits and pieces from the bush and some beads, I had made myself an American Indian healing stick. I then had another vision to make my own dream catcher. I headed out to get the necessities and got started. I was quite pleased with the way the dream catcher had turned out. I put the Indian healing stick and the dream catcher I had made in my bedroom.

Even though I had made the American Indian healing stick, it was scary. I had not touched this healing stick since placing it in the bedroom maybe three months earlier. I walked into the bedroom one day, and happened to pick it up. All of a sudden, I started chanting. I quickly put it back down and thought "What was that?" "Not going there again." But it got the better of me. Every so often, I would pick it up, and every time, I would start chanting.

Over time I kept having this vision of an American Indian healing room and working with the Indians to perform healings. I knew how the healing room had to look. I also knew I should not set the healing room up in the unit that I currently lived in. But every so often, I had a vision of what I needed to do.

My next spiritual experience was not nice. I found myself feeling very edgy over a week. When I pulled up in front of Rayleen's for meditation on the Friday night, I felt like I was having a panic attack. I was a nervous wreck and hoped that no one had noticed when I went in. After a while, I settled down. However, by Saturday, I was a mess. It was like something or someone had control over me. As soon as it became dark, I had to put all the lights on in the unit and not leave, because if I did, I would not go back in - not even to get my belongings. Through the day, it was OK; I was on edge and knew I was not myself. I had work to keep my mind occupied but didn't want to leave work to go home. I knew how I would feel at night. I thought I was going mad and didn't know how to deal with it. I was not in a good place and didn't know why or what had happen to me. What was I going to do, who could I tell, who could I trust, no one will believe me. Then I thought, Rayleen, maybe she won't think I'm mad. So I rang and asked could I come over. I had a major problem and needed help by all means. "Come on over" Rayleen said. As we sat and I explained what was taking place with me. I asked her if I was losing my mind. Trust me, this is not who I am, as I felt so depressed, and I'm not a depressed person at all. I knew Rayleen would be the only person who would understand what I was feeling and trying to say.

Rayleen asked "Why have you not spoken of this earlier?" and asked me a few questions. Rayleen asked if she could give me a healing on the coming Saturday. Rayleen then suggested that Sarita would also be there to help out. I thanked her and we talked for a while. Although I was relieved to be offered some help, I still had to go home to that unit.

When Saturday arrived, I was looking forward to having the healing session. I didn't want to feel this way anymore and anything was worth a try. Upon arriving at Rayleen's house, I was feeling on edge. We started with a smudging which my body didn't like much. I was shaking the whole time. We then headed off to Rayleen's healing room. I knew I would be safe, and put all my trust in Rayleen and Sarita. I lay on the bed and closed my eyes. I was trying to relax, so they could get started. Rayleen had explained exactly what they were about to do. I was not in a good place. It was the dark side and it was trying to pull me back down. I was struggling very hard with this. The struggle went on for quite a while. In the end, I broke through kicking, and saying no, no more, I'm not scared of you. I then felt like I was starting to come into the light. Afterwards, I sat in the healing room for a while trying to gather my thoughts of what had just taken place. I then headed out to the kitchen table to talk with Rayleen and Sarita. While I was drinking water I was talking to them about what had taken place. I could not thank Rayleen and Sarita enough. I was feeling very drained. It was all very strange and I was trying to get my head around what had just taken place. Upon leaving, I hoped into my car and turned on the ignition. My radio was just a high pitched buzzing sound. I couldn't get a radio station at all. I had to get my son to come over the next day to reset the radio. This was very strange or was it?

The healing had worked. I was starting to feel myself again. I think the experience had made me a stronger person. I was still trying to work out what had happened. You hear some people talk of 'entities'. So was it that? I didn't know. But I knew I didn't ever want to feel like that again. Rayleen and Sarita also told me I must smudge myself quite regularly and so I took their advice. Thank you Rayleen and Sarita, from the bottom of my heart.

Sometimes on a Saturday morning my friend, Donna would call in for morning tea. I had spoken of her earlier in this book. Her husband was Gav's mate. Donna knew I was interested in spiritual things and to my surprise, so was she. Donna is a very sweet and shy soul. We would talk for hours on all things spiritually related. I think Donna and I, are definitely past life souls and our bond would grow closer and closer like mother and daughter. When I look in her eyes, I see myself at a younger age.

2009 rolled around and it was another year to get older and wiser. I remember sitting in the staff room at work having lunch. There were a few girls sitting in there having their lunch when the conversation turned on different places we had lived. Jenny, a nurse sitting across from me confirmed every place I had lived in my earlier times; she had lived there to, at the same time. Our paths were just crossing now. I felt the universe didn't want us to meet until now. We became very good friends over time. We started walking in the afternoon to get fit. But we also got to know each other, and our life stories. We laughed how we had never met each other sooner. Jen and I are still good friends, and catch up all the time. Jen is a good soul, with a good heart, and has a lovely partner, Neil. Both Jen and Neil go out of their way, to help whenever or whoever needs help. That's just what they do, with no hesitation, no questions asked.

I remember when Gav, Sarina, Cody, Chloe and Gav's mate Scotto was coming for tea. It was Saturday and the boys were out at Craig's doing some work on the hot rods. Sarina, Cody and Chloe came over earlier. Sarina and I caught up on the latest news, and then started tea. Gav and Scotto arrived about 6pm. I remember Scotto coming into the lounge room with his hands behind his back and said "I have something here for you Di." "What hand would you like?" After choosing a hand, I said "O MY GOD!!! Another American Indian picture!" It was magnificent! It was from Craig. He said he wanted you to have it. I was in the middle of serving up, so I said "Just lean it against the wall in the lounge room and after tea, I will find a spot for it." Scotto was looking around at all my other pictures on the wall then yelled out "Di, why would you want the same Indian twice?" I said "What do you mean?" I came to look and it was the same Indian. I checked a few times to make sure. Go figure that! Over a period of time, two more High Horse Indian pictures came to me. The Indians and universe were trying to get my attention and so I knew my spirit guide was 'High Horse'!

Sitting out the back courtyard of my unit one day, my fascination with crows was unbelievable. I even managed to form a bond with one crow. This crow would come every day. If I was not out the back, he would sit on the little glass table looking through the glass sliding door looking for me. I decided when I could afford to get a tattoo; it would be the name of my spirit guide, High Horse. I asked if I could put my spirit name with his and if so, what my spirit name was. That's when all of a sudden two crows came flying past yelling out, so yes, later down the track I did get that tattoo!"

'High Horse' a picture of a feather then, '2 Crows Flying.'

Crows are a major part of me. I just love them and hear them over anything. Right at this very moment, while I'm writing this, the crows are in very loud in my backyard. Just like they know I am talking about them. *laughs*! I believe they are messengers from God, representing change and new beginnings.

I was learning how the universe worked, what you put out is what you will get in return.

So always remember be a positive person, with positive thoughts, and my biggest one is GRATITUDE.

I recognize that I am driving the universe and creating my own experiences.

Positive thoughts and gratitude works, trust me, not overnight, but it works, just believe!

Happiness is not something
ready-made
It comes from your own actions

Dalai Lama

I remember being home washing up from tea one night when Mum rang. She was down staying with her sister, June. Mum and June loved being together, but this was a sad phone call. Mum was upset and I could tell. I asked Mum "What is the matter?" Mum said Sharyn had just phoned and said she would have to find somewhere to live, as Sharyn was moving out of town into a shed. Mum had been living with Sharyn and her family for years. Mum was upset. Mum and I both cried, but I remember Mum saying "Don't cry, I will be fine." That was Mum, always caring for everyone else. It didn't matter how she felt.

After leaving her sister, June, Mum travelled to stay with me for a few weeks. I remember we would sit for hours out the back on weekends and talk. It was always nice to come home from work and have a cuppa ready for you. Mum kept herself busy in the unit tinkering or having a shut eye while watching a DVD. I remember one morning getting up early to make a coffee and heading outside into the courtyard. Out came Mum to tell me she had the fright of her life last night. Mum said she had woken up through the night to see a little girl standing at the side of her bed. I said "What did you do?" Mum said "I pulled the sheets over my head and was shitting myself." I could not stop laughing.

I always told Mum the fairies used to come and visit me often. Outside in front of my bedroom window, there would be a collection of mushrooms. My unit was the only one with mushrooms out of the fifty units in the complex. I always told myself, I was blessed to have the fairies visit.

Mum then headed over to Peta and Ged's home for a while. Mum loved being there. Mum just loved being with Peta and her family. Mum always said there was no one like them. It felt like home. Just between you and me, I think she hangs out there all the time now, but that will be our secret.

Determined to get a place of her own, Mum started collecting the things she would need. I was worried, at her age, about moving into a unit by herself. How would Mum cope with being lonely? I know better than anyone, when you shut that door and you are on your own, life is not good. It can very lonely.

Kristy was trying to get a unit in Wauchope, not far from where she lived. Kristy had a special bond with Mum and Dad. Kristy lived with Mum and Dad for twelve months when she was little. When Dad passed away Kristy and Peta's bond with Mum was something special. Kristy and Peta were Mum's guardian angels. Kristy organised Mum a little unit. Mum was excited about the unit. It was up on a hill amongst a nice block of units. Most of the people living in the block of units were around Mum's age. So Mum headed back to Wauchope and set herself up in the unit. We would ring each other and catch up once a week. I remember one day, Mum rang all excited and said "Di, the fairies are here outside my window." "Just like your place." See Mum, you just have to believe.

Kristy was always there for Mum. Mum would go down to Kirsty's for the day. Sharyn called in occasionally. Mum would always say Kristy was her beacon of light. Mum settled in well. Even Gav had headed that way with his car carrying business to drop off a car and called in and had tea with Mum. Mum was excited to have Gav there for tea. Gav said that her unit was lovely.

It was a week before Easter and Mum had taken sick and was admitted to hospital. Peta rang and made arrangements to pick me up on her way through. Peta and I were heading down over the Easter break to see Mum in hospital, as Mum was not good. Peta, Megan and I stayed at Kirsty's during this time.

Mum got well enough to go home, but slowly Mum's health deteriorated. I remember Kristy, Mum and my friend Kathy, had flown up for two weeks' holiday. When I meet them at the airport, Mum came out in a wheelchair. I didn't notice how bad Mum was, till we got home. Kristy helped Mum to shower and dress as she struggled to breathe. This was not the Mum I knew. Even Kathy had said how bad Mum was.

Peta came and stayed the night. Mum and Peta had made a decision that Mum was going to stay with Peta for a while, instead of going back to her unit. So Peta and Mum headed back to Kingaroy. Kristy and her children packed up Mum's unit. For Kristy it was sad, as she wouldn't get to see Mum as much.

Mum's health deteriorated. Poor Peta was dealing with it all. I felt bad as it should have been me. Sharyn decided to give Peta a break and get Mum into respite at a nursing home. That was not good for Mum, as Mum had a fall and took a massive piece out of her leg. When Peta arrived at the nursing home, Mum was lying in a wet bed, which had been wet all night with no treatment. Peta pulled Mum straight out of the nursing home and took Mum to the nearest hospital.

Mum slowly got worse. It was a lot of work for Peta and their family, but they never complained. Mum ended up with what they call 'Sundowner'. Mum didn't sleep at night. Peta wasn't game to shut her eyes, as she would not have known what Mum was up to. Peta was worried Mum would have a fall during the night.

A decision had been made, which I know would have been one of Peta's hardest decisions in this life time. Mum had to go into a nursing home. It was becoming too much. Mum needed to have twenty four hour care. Mum had to be assessed to see if Mum was high or low care. We had spoken to the Director of Nursing, but it was a waiting game to get a bed. Peta got lucky and was able to get Mum into a nursing home near her home. This was very hard on Peta, as Peta felt like she had failed Mum. I felt like I was failing both of them. I couldn't do anything. I was in a unit, just making enough money to cover my own expenses. I had to work and couldn't look after my own mum. I felt bad and it made me feel like I was passing all my responsibility onto Peta. I was suffering in silence, and worried what my own family must think of me. Not being able to take care of my own mother.

Peta and Ged got Mum settled into the nursing home. Gav, Sarina, Cody, Chloe and I went over on the weekend and stayed at Peta's house. We all went in and had the afternoon with Mum. Peta had her room looking beautiful. Peta kept me up to date and always made sure Mum had everything.

The saddest and hardest thing was when Eileen, who was the Director of Nursing, at the nursing home where I worked, came and saw me because someone had passed and there was now a high care room available. Now I thought I was doing the right thing by bringing Mum closer to me in Brisbane. But honestly, what was I doing to Peta who had done everything for Mum, when I couldn't. The ambulance that was bringing Mum turned up early. Peta then had to chase the ambulance down the highway, to stop it, to say goodbye to Mum. I can't even begin to think what that was like, or what Peta was feeling. I just hope that one day in her heart, she will understand why I did it, and forgive me.

Mum got settled in. I never really knew with Mum what was right or wrong, but we made the most of our time together. I must have picked her room when I first started working at the nursing home. All the people before Mum in that room, I had formed a bond with. On my way to the nursing home to collect the washing, I would wave to them, as they sat at their window. It was a perfect room and now it was Mum's room. I could go visit before work, during my work day, and after work. On the weekends, the family loved going there to. Mum was in room 93 and across from her in room 92, a beautiful lady had moved in. Her name was Agnus and got my attention. As soon as Agnus moved in, on her wall were American Indian pictures, so we got talking.

Another year down and heading into 2010. I'd been in Brisbane four years now. Mum had been in the nursing home for eight weeks. June, her sister Chris, and Sue had come to visit. June stayed with me for a few days and Mum loved having them there. Without knowing this, it was their last goodbyes. You know how they say that that person will try and wait to see all of the family. Well I have a sister in Cairns, so I guess Mum was hanging in there hoping she would come and visit and she did for a couple of hours. Mum was happy to see her, and if Mum was happy, so were we.

Now the universe works in wonderful ways and trust me one afternoon after work there was a knock at my front door. It was Judy, the caretaker. Judy said "Di, are you interested in taking in a boarder." There are three girls currently in a unit but have to leave. One of these girls would like to stay and is looking for a room to rent, so I thought of you. I asked Judy what she was like. Judy said that she seemed nice and that she was tidy. I agreed to have a chat to her.

Her name was also Di. Di was looking for a room to rent which I happened to have. She could have her own bathroom and toilet, as I had an ensuite. I thought that this might just work and give me extra money. I decided to give this a go. I spent a lot of weekends with Mum, so that was fine. But let's just say without been rude, it was just not working out big time. We were two different personalities and very different people. I just didn't realise at that time why she had been brought to me, so I persisted as long as I could, but I was struggling big time.

One afternoon, I was sitting out in my back courtyard of the unit, when these words started coming to me. I couldn't work out why. I got some writing paper and started writing down the poem; 'I Am Free.'

Dianne Crows

I Am Free

Don't be sad, for I am free.

The Angels are here there holding me.

Don't be sad, for I am free.

The Angels are here and they're guiding me.

Their wings so soft, as they wrap around me.

I feel blessed where they are taking thee.

I see the light, it is so white.

Don't be sad, for I am free.

The music is soft, as I reach the gate.

OH MY GOD, look where they are taking me.

It's Allen, Dennis, Mum and Dad.

They've all been here waiting for me.

I'm not scared, for I am safe.

The Angels have taken me to a blessed place.

So watch for the feather that catches your eye.

And just remember it's me passing by.

Don't be sad, for I am free.

Always remember, I love each and every one of thee.

Nothing can bring you

peace but yourself

Ralph Waldo Emerson

O MY GOD! I have just written a poem for my mum. What was wrong with me?

I went to meditation on the Friday night and told them of what I had just written. The people at the mediation group said that it was beautiful. They told me that I was being prepared for the time that was coming. They said that maybe I was meant to read it.

Six weeks later, that time did come. I had spoken to Agnus on the Tuesday. I told Agnus of my spirit guide High Horse, and the beautiful pictures I had of him. Agnus asked if she could see them. I told her, I would bring the pictures in the next day. So when I got home, I took down two pictures of High Horse and told High Horse that he was coming to work tomorrow to meet a lovely lady. On Wednesday morning I woke up early and was at work by 5am. I was in the laundry, when my guide got into my head reminding me that the pictures were still out in the car. I went out and brought the pictures into where I worked. I thought to myself, I hope no one is watching, they will think I am mad. After about ten minutes, my guide was in my head again, saying "You have to go to the nursing home now." So I picked up the pictures and headed up. I opened Agnus's door and creeped in. I put the pictures against the wall at the end of her bed, but she woke up. "It's just me, Agnes." I said. I have brought in my pictures for you. When you wake up later, and it's light, you will see them. "Thank you." Agnus said. I gave Agnus a kiss and told her to go back to sleep.

Then in an instant, my guide said "Go straight to your mother now." "OK" I thought. "No, I mean, now." So I shut Agnus's door and went across to Mum's room. Mum was sleeping and looked so beautiful, like never before. Mum looked at peace. So I put my hand under her head, lifted it up and gave her a kiss. I said "I love you." "I will be back later to visit." I kissed her again, shut her door and returned to the laundry.

About thirty minutes later, Nancy, a Registered Nurse, walked into the laundry. I dropped to my knees. I knew what she had come to say, as she had never visited the laundry before. Nancy and I walked back to the nursing home. I was struggling to see where I was going. I was wiping the tears from my face. Nancy asked "Would you like me to come in with you?" I said "No, thank you, I will be fine." As I slowly opened the door, there laid my mum. She was still beautiful, just like before, so at peace. I gave her my last kiss and said "In the arms of the angels, I love you." Holding Mum's hand with so many thoughts running through my head, Nancy then came back into the room to check on Mum. Nancy said I had to make sure, as I had never seen anyone so at peace. Mum still looked like she was sleeping. I was struggling over time. I moved from the bed to the chair talking to her. Then from the chair to her chest of drawers and lend on them. I then moved from the chest of drawers to the door. You see, once I opened that door and left, that was it. My mum would be gone. I had lost my dad, my brother and now my mum.

I walked outside and just couldn't function. What to do? Who do I ring? Think, think, think. How was I going to tell Peta and Kristy? Mum was a very important person in their life. Mum had just died and they were not there to say goodbye.

After making a few phone calls, I headed home. I paced, as I didn't know what to do, or feel. I felt empty inside. I headed out into the back courtyard, sitting there crying. I looked up to the sky and said "Mum, please, all I need to know is that you're happy." "That you are finally with Dad." Not long after, a feather came floating down. I wiped my tears and said "Thank you Mum, Thank you."

Mum was very clever; you see she died on the Wednesday. It was Easter that weekend, so we wouldn't be able to have a funeral before the following Wednesday. This would give all the family time to get there. You see that was my mum, always thinking of everyone else. Angel Peta organised it all. Tee-arna did the tribute and it was absolutely amazing. I still pull out the DVD and watch it. The service was lovely and all the children got up and talked. We were very proud of them. Sarina did Mum's ullage. God bless her, she struggled all the way through it. Gav stood by her side, to give her strength. Just before it was my turn to read this poem I had written, I felt Mum run her hands over me. I stopped crying and all of a sudden, felt a sense of peace. Mum was giving me the strength to do what I needed to. We all ended back at the Greenbank RSL for drinks and tea. It was lovely and beautiful to be with all the family on such a sad day. Rayleen, from meditation group, had come to the funeral and then came back to the club with the rest of the family. I really appreciated Rayleen being there for me.

I always found it hard being with all the family. They would have to leave at some point, but this time, it was different, as I had no one. A nurse had told me the night before Mum had died that Mum said she was tied and had had enough and wanted to go! The nurse said it's OK, if you need to go! But Mum said she was worried about me. Everybody had somebody but I had nobody. The nurse told her, that I would be fine. I was big enough and ugly enough to take care of myself. But you know what, I wasn't. After everyone left on Thursday, I cleaned up to keep busy. The cleaning soon came to an end. I went up to have a shower and sat on the shower floor crying. I was all alone and I didn't have anybody. Mum was right. Sure I had my son, but he had his family now and they were his priority. But after about ten minutes crying in the shower, Mum worked her magic again. I turned the shower off, dried myself and said "You can do this." "Just because you can't see Mum, doesn't mean she is not there." Mum will always be there, especially when things get tough. Mum always is there. She always leaves me a calling card, just to confirm it, a feather. Time heals all they say, but my heart sure had taken a beaten.

So you know what I had said earlier about my boarder living with me, and why was she there. You see the universe brought this person to me, when I was in need. I had to help pay for Mum's funeral. The money my boarder was paying me, helped to pay for the funeral. My boarder moved out not long after. The universe works in wonderful ways, trust me, just believe and always feel with your heart.

It was time to get up and dust myself off and get on with my life. I was becoming a stronger person. I thank my mediation group for that.

In June 2010, Peta, Kristy, Sharyn and I travelled to Orange with Mum's ashes to put them with Dad. This is what Mum wanted. Megan couldn't make it with us. We felt like we were on a road trip with Mum again and were having the best time. We all stayed at my friend Kathy's place. It was a great trip. We even had our own little service at the cemetery, as we placed Mum's ashes with Dad.

Gav was going along well with building the hot rod. It was looking really good. I was very proud of him and the man he had become. Gav was a very good father. He loved his children and his wife. But he will always be my little boy.

At the beginning of 2011, my grandson, Cody was growing up and starting school. Cody was so tiny with glasses, in a school uniform. He looked so cute. I was fighting back the tears. I had asked the universe to please take very good care of this little boy during his school years. To keep him safe, protected and to help him to make the right choices. Where had time gone! It felt like yesterday that Gav was going to school for the first time. Now, it was my grandson. God love him.

My meditation group had finished. I had done so much healing, and learnt what I needed to. It had been four years now and it was time to stand on my own. I thank them from the bottom of my heart. My friendship with Rayleen ended, but I will always remember what Rayleen had done for me. They say people come in and out of your life for a reason. I will always be grateful for being part of the mediation group.

My unit where I lived was still the same. I was still been harassed at night, but I was slowly standing up for myself. I started to put it out to the universe, for a house, in a good street, with good neighbors.

A very safe house with a beautiful kitchen, a good size covered deck out the back and a beautiful healing room for the Indians. I would say positive affirmations about this and my vision board had a lovely home on it. The seeds were being planted.

I started smelling spirit for the first time. When I first started, I didn't know what it was. I remember being with Carol at a large department store and as we walked out I said "O, Can you smell that?" She replied "Smell what?" I said "That stench, it's making me sick." It was so strong. It happened quite a few times. Carol told me I was losing it. The smell was like when you roll up a wet old style tent and then get it out six months later. The smell was like a really strong smell of mould. It was driving me mad. I remember Carol and I had gone to the club on a Saturday night. It was a good night of dancing and laughing. The band had stopped and the lead singer was talking about their next song. All of a sudden that stench was there, but this time, it was so strong. As I turned around, there were two guys standing behind me, and I felt cold. I don't know why, but I felt like they had just done something or were about to. I was feeling sick, so Carol and I left. That smell stopped, after a while, and changed to perfume and wood. Often at night while watching TV, it was a power struggle with the wood and perfume fighting to get my attention. I would have to yell "Enough is enough." "I know you are both there, but seriously, I'm trying to watch my TV program."

Sometimes, I get woken up at night to the smell of perfume. It's so strong. I have a coughing fit. But, I guess, they're just letting me know that they are visiting.

Yesterday is gone

Tomorrow has not come

We have only today

Let us begin

Mother Teresa

I was feeling very stuck with my life. I felt like I really needed to do something. I needed a holiday of some sort. But how could I afford this? Then it hit me. Gav was the answer. I approached Gav and asked was there any chance of getting a bit of my invested money out of the hot rod, as I would love a holiday. Gav said that was not a problem. I was very excited about the possibility of a holiday in 2012. I rang my friend Kathy. We spoke in detail on the phone of a holiday. We had always wanted to see Ireland and the UK. Kathy was all in. In my wildest dreams, I never thought I would go past Sydney.

Kathy and I were making arrangements to fly to Dubai, stay the night, then off to London for two days. We then joined a bus tour to see right up to Scotland then back down across to Ireland. We then went back across to travel down through Wales, Brighton then back to London for a few more days. After that we then went back to Dubai for a week. Someone pinch me, but 2012 would slowly change my life. I had now something else to focus on. My friend Carol was in her glory, helping me arrange it all. We booked the flights, organised passports and sorted out what needed to be packed. We were flying out May, 1 and returning on June, 2. I had eight months to plan and organise it all.

Around October 2011, I was at work pulling linen out of one of the washing machines, when I felt my shoulder tear. The pain was horrendous, but I shrugged it off and kept working. It got worse. I thought I had pulled a muscle in my shoulder or neck. That's where the pain was. I headed off to the doctors and he had said the same thing, just a muscle strain. The doctor told me to rest over the weekend and it will be fine. By Monday, I could hardly work; I was in so much pain. One of the Registered Nurses at work checked my shoulder and said it was full of fluid. I needed to go back to the doctors, only this time, I went to another doctor. The X-ray ultra sound showed I had done damage. I would be off work for a few weeks, to rest it. The doctor told me I was wasting my time; Work cover will not cover me. It could be just a frozen shoulder more or less, suck it up and get over it. But now it was getting worse over time. My chiropractor told me I needed to see a specialist. I arranged an appointment with a specialist in February 2012. Until then, I just had to put up with it and live on pain killers.

I worked over Christmas 2011, as I had done the previous two Christmas'. Gav, Sarina, Cody and Chloe were all heading to Orange for Christmas that year. My Christmas was pretty quiet. Although, I didn't mind the extra pay from working on the public holidays.

I was excited when 2012 finally arrived. It was only four months until my holiday.

When February 2012 came, I went to see the specialist. The specialist sent me for an MRI, to see the actual damage, and to make sure it wasn't a frozen shoulder. By the time, I got the MRI, and then went back to the specialist to discuss the results, it was late March. The news was not good; I had torn my shoulder bad. The specialist advised that I was not able to have key hole surgery. I would have to be cut. The specialist had to get approval from Workcover to make sure I was covered. I informed the specialist that I was going overseas in May. I booked another appointment for April. In April I was told that I was covered by Workcover. The specialist would book me in for surgery as soon as I came back from my holiday. I was informed by the specialist, that I would get a letter, letting me know when the surgery would be.

I kept busy working during the lead up to my holiday. Cody and Chloe were coming over for sleepovers on the weekends. I was also sorting out clothes to take on my holidays. Peta had brought me new travel bags for my birthday. I was very grateful for the travel bags. Peta always spoils me. This year was definitely going to be big. It was the change I needed in my life.

The time had finally arrived for my holiday. Kathy was flying up from Sydney on a Tuesday afternoon and we would fly out from Brisbane that same night. Our flight was at 11.30pm and Gav would drop us off. I was nervous, as well as excited. I'm not very good on planes and this was a big one. I was petrified on take offs and landings. It started off good, although, my first drink I spilt all over myself. Orange juice on white pants, not a good look! Sitting for the first twelve hours, was not that comfortable, but we did have a few laughs. My holiday was everything and more that I could have asked for. UK was breath taking. I loved the buildings, history, and the people. The bus trip over the month was mind blowing with wonderful people. We made amazing friends and Kathy and I ended up with the name Kath and Kim. They said we keep them laughing the whole trip. We saw some wonderful things and were told great stories.

Now as you can imagine four weeks on the road and the amount of motels we had stayed at. The accommodation and meals were really good. But I will share one of my stories with you. This is between you and me and no one else. There were no keys just swipe cards at each of the accommodation places. As you got off the bus at each motel; you were given your card to your room. The room numbers changed from 112 to room 503 to 60 to 142 to 90 at each motel we stayed at. So you can see, you begin to forget, where you are up to. By the third week or so we had stopped for the day. It was about 3pm in the afternoon and most of the people on the bus tour were off to see the sights of the town. Kathy and I had decided to stay back and just relax. Kathy and I were down at the bar when Kathy said she was heading outside for a smoke. I said I really needed to go to the toilet. So we agreed that we would meet back at the bar shortly. I said "Room 124, that's our room." Kathy replied "Yep, for sure." So I headed off, but when I got to the door my card would not work. I thought this may have happened quite a bit. I really needed to go to the toilet, badly. I hurried back to reception and told the girl about the card. The receptionist apologised and cut me two new ones. I quickly ran back to room 124. Mind you, just making it back in time to the room! While sitting on the toilet, thinking of the things I had seen that day, I was thinking to myself, my lips are so dry and I need to put some lip balm on. When I finished, I flushed the toilet, washed my hands and headed out to the bedroom to get my toiletries bag. I stopped in my tracks saying "f*** f*** f***, this is not our room." I quickly ran to the door to get out. All I could visualize was the people in this room standing on the other side of the door. How would I ever explain myself being in their room? I opened the door and ran for my life to the lift. As the lift door opened, there was Kathy saying that is not our room. That is not our room, well it's too late. I have just shit in their toilet. We both could not stop laughing. We kept that secret, only sharing with a handful of people.

If someone had said to me two years earlier, you will head overseas to see some amazing things and met some amazing people, I would have said "Yeah, in your dreams." But you see this was on my vision board. So your dreams do come true. You just have to put it out there.

One friendship Kathy and I formed on our holiday was with Jocelyn. Jocelyn and I are still good friends and catch up all the time. Jocelyn is one of the most caring souls you could meet, and always loves a good laugh. I remember when the bus trip had come to the end in London and everyone was saying their goodbyes. We couldn't find Jocelyn to say goodbye. We asked her mum for which her mum replied "She is still on the bus crying." "She didn't want us to leave." That's Jocelyn's soft and sweet nature.

When I came home, I had a suitcase full of gifts for the family. It was like Christmas and we told all our stories. Kathy stayed for more two days then headed home to her family.

Upon arriving back home, I received a letter saying that I was being operated on June, 8. I went back to work for two days, then was off work for three more months. I learnt fast how to do everything with one hand. I was by myself and was determined to get my shoulder working properly. I wanted to get back to work as fast as I could.

During my last two weeks off work, I headed to Peta's house to stay for a few days. Megan, Peta's sister was living at Nanango. We wanted to catch up as Megan loved the spiritual side of life as much as I did.

We talked for hours. We also headed out to the lavender farm about 1km out of Kingaroy for morning tea. It had an amazing gift shop with all things made with lavender. As we were walking into the shop, there were some beautiful little rabbits on a table. I stopped and picked one up. I was attracted to it and said to Megan, I'm going to buy this on my way out. Megan said "What for?" I replied "Because I just have to have it." So I purchased it on the way out.

Three weeks later, my niece Kristy rang. Kristy told me she had found two amazing pictures of American Indians at a garage sale and had brought them for me. Kristy said she would send them up with Peta, as she was heading down that way. So I thanked her and was excited to see these pictures. A month later, Peta called in on her way back from Kristy's home, to stay the night and drop off the pictures. The pictures were amazing. There was something about the people in the pictures. His eyes follow you and she was beautiful. In one of the pictures, an American Indian girl is leaning on a tree with a rabbit. What was mind blowing was, it was the same looking rabbit I brought a few months earlier. My connections with American Indians were getting stronger and stronger.

Agnus, who was across from Mum's room, had given me a book 'Bury My Heart at Wounded Knee' by Dee Brown. Agnus had asked her family to buy the book for me. Inside the book she wrote 'To Dianne, I hope this will help you, Love Agnus.' What a beautiful and amazing woman Agnus was. I visited Agnus until she passed away at the age of 94. I had a connection with Agnus and feel I must have had a past life with her.

The best way to predict the

future is to create it

Abraham Lincoln

We were heading for another Christmas. Work was going good and my shoulder was getting back to normal.

At the beginning of 2013, I had another grandchild starting school. My little Chloe was growing up. To see Chloe in a school uniform made me so proud. I had a tear in my eye and I asked the universe once again to watch over her and keep her safe and guide her. But Chloe is different to Cody. Chloe won't let anyone put anything over her and stands up for herself. I knew she would be fine.

Peta had rung to say Tee-arna had applied for University in Brisbane. Tee-arna was waiting to hear back to see if she was accepted. Peta asked if she could stay with me during this time. Tee-arna ended up being accepted into the University. In the last week of February we went to the University for Tee-arna to register. After that we went and brought her a study desk, chair and a chest of drawers. Unfortunately, the desk, chair and drawers were all flat packed and we had to put it all together. That was a night and a half, full of laughs!

I remember Tee-arna's first afternoon to start university. I was driving to drop Tee-arna off at the bus stop, when we got a horrific storm. Tee-arna and I both panicked and were saying if it floods Tee-arna will get stuck. Tee-arna and I talked ourselves into turning around and coming back home. The storm stopped twenty minutes later. Tee-arna never got to her first day of University. We were off to a good start together, as we were both as bad as each other *laughs*.

Tee-arna got a part time job at a newsagency in a nearby shopping plaza. She headed back home on most weekends, as she had a boyfriend that lived at Murgan. You know when your young and in love, that rules over everything. Tee-arna's boyfriend was quite a nice guy. Tee-arna and I had some good girl talks, while doing the dishes at night.

But, poor Tee-arna! I woke up one night about 2.30am to see Tee-arna's light still on. I thought Tee-arna had fallen asleep. I got up and headed down to turn off the light. I found Tee-arna sitting up in bed. Tee-arna said she had been woken up to a man standing at her doorway watching her. Tee-arna was scared stiff. This happened quite a bit. Most times she would sleep with the light on. I had told her about what would happen to me and often woke up thinking, there was someone standing at the side of my bed. I had got used to it, and couldn't stand the light on.

I think that was a turning point. I had made my mind up. I was moving that year. I wanted out of there, so I downloaded the real estate app. I started looking for rentals. I still had a lot of things packed in boxes, which I couldn't put out in my unit. I needed to find a house to rent and a yard for the grandchildren to play. Gav had finished the hot rod and sold it, and repaid my investment, which made it easier to move. I had had enough now. Every time my visitors came into my room, I would sit up and yell "This is my unit, my space, if you don't like it, please leave."

I remember one night Chloe was sleeping over. Up the hallway they came running into my room. I thought, no way. I'm not putting up with this while my granddaughter, was in the room with me. Chloe looked sound asleep. I sat up and said "By the order of the universe, go to light and repeated it and they left." The next morning Sarina had called over to pick up Chloe. We sat out in the courtyard and had a cuppa. Chloe was playing when she said out of the blue "Nan had visitors last night, but she told them to go to the light." O MY GOD! I thought she was sound asleep. I said "So sorry Sarina." Sarina replied "No, that's fine Mum."

It also seems Chloe has a gift too. Chloe was at home in bed one night and started yelling out. Gav jumped out of bed and ran to her. Chloe said "That man?" Gav replied, "What man?" Gav was in a panic looking around everywhere. Chloe said "At the end of my bed." "The man keeps turning my music off." Gav turned her music back on and settled her down, then returned to Sarina. Gav said to Sarina "Chloe is going to do all that shit Mum does." I laughed when Sarina told me.

In May 2013, Kathy had headed back up to spend two weeks with me. I was picking her up from her Aunty Ed's place. We were heading to the Gold Coast for a week and Tee-arna was staying in the unit by herself. Luckily Shannon was coming over two days later. We had a wonderful two weeks, as I always do with Kathy. Kathy is my twin flame best friend. I love being with Kathy. I hope that one day I can find the same qualities in Kathy, as I do in a man. If that makes sense! Kathy and I started planning our next trip, for the following year, maybe a cruise.

Tee-arna had decided to do university online and head back and live with Shannon. I think Tee-arna had had enough of me and my unit *laughs*. Tee-arna has done well for herself. She is still doing university, along with working, and her relationship with Shannon is good.

Now you know what they say, you have to make things happen. So I started packing up the unit and putting everything into one room while I was looking for a house to rent. But every house I had looked at was, two steps in, and ten steps back to the car. The houses I looked at for rent were feral. I don't know how other people can rent them. I had started to notice one real estate had quite tidy properties. So I was looking at a lot of available homes to rent there. There are a lot of people looking to rent and about thirty people were turning up to each open house. Since, I was by myself; I was worried about who was going to give me a house, when there were families looking to rent. But I found a secret. If I liked one; I completed the rental application form, before I had a look. That way, I could hand the rental application form in, as I was leaving the open house.

My flat was packed up and I had no house to move to. I was beginning to worry. Had I made a mistake? Then it happened. I had spotted this house in Regents Park. It looked perfect. It was a Monday afternoon inspection. I was first there sitting in my car. The yard looked lovely and the street looked good. I thought to myself "Mmm, we will see." As the inspection started, people came in droves. But as I stepped into this house, it was as though the house reached out and put its arms around me. It was all that I was looking for and more. I was in love with this home, but what was my chance? As I handed my form in upon leaving the inspection, the lady from the real estate commented that I was keen. I told the real estate that I sure was keen.

I knew I was running out of time. My lease was running out soon and they would want me to sign a new one. By the Wednesday, I had not heard from the real estate. They usually got back to you in two days, so I thought I had missed out.

I had arrived home Thursday and was making a cuppa when my phone rang. "Dianne, it's the Real Estate." To my surprise she said "I just rang to congratulate you, the house is yours." I was so excited. I told her that I would call into the real estate the next day and do all the paper work and could move in on August, 23. It was a Friday and I could get the day off work. That will give me the weekend to get settled. I could finally give notice in the unit. Thank you universe, Thank you! I was beside myself. Smile from ear to ear. The next day I took myself for a drive pass to have another look. I was pleased that my new home would only be four minutes' drive to work.

The day arrived when I was able to collect the keys to my new home and finally move in. Unfortunately, my family was all working and no one was able to help me move. I was used to doing things all by myself, so I packed up the remainder of my unit. I was lucky enough, that my good friend, Jenny offered to help with a Ute.

I spent my last night in that unit sleeping on the lounge room floor. I was glad to hear the alarm at 5am. I had put up with living in this horrible unit for seven years. I had been through a lot and grown enormously. I had learnt a lot of lessons. On the morning of the move I packed my car to the brim. Jen arrived with the Ute to take the beds and mattresses and any boxes in the gaps. We then headed off to my new home.

I opened the front door to my new home and it felt like the home had hands wrapping around me again. I was so excited and felt right at home. Jenny said how beautiful it was, as we walked through and looked around. O MY GOD! Look at your back deck. It is amazing! I knew I would spend a lot of time out on the back deck, relaxing with a coffee. The first spare bedroom had a pink feature wall and I knew this would be the spare guests' room. Then the next spare bedroom had a purple feature wall, and I knew this was going to be my Indian healing room. Jen said it was perfect. My kitchen was big and spacious and looked into the lounge room. I had a beautiful main bedroom and bathroom. I loved it!!! Jen and I never stopped all day. We had many trips back and forth. I could not thank her enough. Jen was wonderful. Thank you Jen, from the bottom of my heart! All that was left was the lounge, fridge and TV unit. Gav brought it after work, with the help of his friend, Kalvin. Jen and I had set up the bed, so at least I could go to bed that night. After a short time out for Chloe's birthday on the Saturday, I then continued with the unpacking into my new home.

I felt very tired after moving and unpacking all weekend. I ached from head to toe, for a week. I had worked so hard, but got it all done. My new home looked good and I was very happy.

I am grateful for my beautiful
home, in a beautiful street,
with beautiful neighbours

Once I had finished the setting up of the living areas of my new home, I was on a mission to setup my healing room. This was done with pride and help from the Indians, on how they would like it to be. It looked amazing! All the things I had made, the gifts I had been given and the things that had been brought. It was coming together. I could feel the energy of the healing room. Everyone that visited my home was amazed at the healing room. It was perfect! My house was perfect! It was a house of serenity and peace and calm. I was feeling at peace myself. I was really protected here and thank the universe for a beautiful home, in a beautiful street, with beautiful neighbours. A beautiful safe house! Thank you, Thank you, Thank you! I found myself in this healing room talking all the time. I share everything with the Indians, from the type of day I had, to a good weekend. I bet they're glad when I walk out *laughs*.

It was November and I had been in my new home for three months. I had been talking to Megan about my healing room. Megan said she would like to come over and bring Lyndal with her on a Saturday to catch up. Megan wanted to try out my American Indian healing room. It sounded like a good idea. We decided to catch up in a fortnights' time. I got in touch with Donna and asked if she would like to come to. I was excited, as well as nervous, on the Saturday. The girls were coming from Kingaroy and Donna was joining us as well. It was one of my most memorable spiritual days. The girls loved my new home and said my healing room was amazing. Megan did some psychic card readings, which she was good at. A gift of reading cards, she chooses not to pursue. I started my healings, explaining this is my first time. I didn't know what to expect. I asked if they would please bear with me, and give honest feedback. Megan was first. As I started, I put her into a relaxing state. I looked at my Indians and said "Let's do this." With my Indian music playing, I started to chant. It was mind blowing; this was not me, where was it coming from. I loved it and I was shown what to do. Megan loved it and said it was wonderful. One by one, each person had a healing. Everyone left after lunch. Megan phoned that afternoon, to say she was still being affected by it and loved it. Megan said "I was amazing." I replied "No, I'm not, the Indians are." I'm just doing what they have asked. They have chosen me to have this gift and I love it.

It was time to give my healing room a name. As I sat with the Indians, I asked "What shall we call this amazing healing room." There it was "Surrender to the Indians." It was perfect in every way. I loved the name. So Donna assisted with registering my business name and organising an Australian Business Number, along with ordering business cards. It was very exciting. I felt the vision was coming together; the Indians had been waiting a very long time for this.

To finish off a good year, Donna and I went to the Sunshine Coast, for a three day Angel Intuitive workshop with Doreen Virtue. I loved every minute of being with like-minded spiritual people. It was amazing!

I was feeling very grateful and happy at the beginning of 2014. I was looking forward to what the year would bring. I lived in a good street, with good neighbours and a beautiful house. I felt like I was the luckiest girl in the world. I was looking forward to heading out on a cruise in May 2014 with my best friends.

Now remember that book I had been given by Agnus 'Bury My Heart at Wounded Knee'. It was time to read it. I felt I needed to read it to the Indians. Why do you ask? I don't know. But that's exactly what I had to do. I would go and lay in this beautiful relaxing lounge I brought for the healing room. The trouble was I could only read a few pages at a time. Every time I read the book, I was crying and yelling at the Indians, saying "I told you they were bastards, but you just wouldn't listen." Sometimes, I was so upset; I just couldn't go any further. It took me nearly a year to read this book. That was how much I struggled with it. I felt like, I was there, every time I would read it. I was given this book for a reason, and trust me there was a lot of healing and love in that room. I can't explain the love and how I feel for these guys. But I know they have given me this gift, so we could work together. I believe that Surrender to the Indians, is a wonderful healing experience to all those that come to this amazing healing room and feel its energy.

I have been given some amazing gifts for this healing room. I remember watching TV one afternoon and there was a documentary on crystals. Turquoise is one of the Indian's stones. The other fascinating crystal was a 'Cherokee Indian Tear Rose'. An old legend says the rose rock represents the blood of the brave, and the tears of the maidens who made the devastating trail of tears journey in the 1800s to Oklahoma. A very sad time! I thought I had a nice turquoise piece, so of I headed to look for it. I found where it was and took the turquoise into the healing room and told the Indians that this is where it belongs. About one hour later my niece, Megan, rang for a catch up. During the conversation she said I have a message for you. I said "O yeah, what's that." Megan replied "The Indians just said thank you so much, for the beautiful piece you just gave them." "The Indians love it." Megan was not sure what it meant and asked if it meant something to me. I said "O MY GOD! Yes." I told her what I had done.

May 2014 arrived and I was on holidays. I headed to Sydney for a few days, then out on a cruise. We stayed in a beautiful unit, and had a great time in Sydney. We visited the zoo, saw some great beaches, and went out for tea. It was good to be with good friends. On the Friday, we headed to the Pacific Jewel Cruise Ship. I questioned myself about going on a cruise, as I was always the one holding the bags at the show, while everyone else was on the rides. I avoided the rides at shows, as I knew, I would be sick. Yet here I was boarding a ship, heading out to the islands. Seriously, what was I thinking?

Did I enjoy? Let's say this. I saw some amazing places, beautiful islands and crystal clear breathtaking water. The food was delicious. But the cruise had seven meter swells, so I was sick. Once I got the right tablets, I was good. But after a while, I found it boring. I'm happy with my both feet firmly on the ground. Even being an Aquarius, I love water and swimming, but not on a cruise. The cruise was definitely not for me.

I went back to work to make some money to pay the bills. I had come up with an idea while I was folding washing one day that I would round up a few girls and see if they were interested in having a psychic reading, on a Saturday, at my place. I had this lady on my Facebook page Donagh Marquard from the Sunshine Coast. I was not sure what she was like, but thought I would get in touch, and see if she was interested. After a few back and forth messages, Donagh was booked. What I thought would start with about six or seven girls, ended up being fourteen. Donagh's psychic readings were amazing and the girls loved her. I don't know how she kept going all day, but she did. I kept the snacks and coffee coming, and I can't imagine how drained she was after a day like that. I guess she was used to it. After everyone left, I sat on the lounge to rest. I was worn out myself.

Donagh came back a few months later, after some of the girls wanted a full one hour psychic reading. This time it was only five girls and Donagh had brought me an amazing American Indian head piece for my healing room. I loved it and so did the Indians. I did a quick healing on Donagh in the lunch break in between readings, to show her what I do. It was a wonderful day, so if any of you are heading to Maroochydore and would like a reading, give Donagh a call. It will be worth it. I will let you in on another secret. If it wasn't for Donagh this book would of never have been written. I would have thought; I was not capable of writing a book. But Donagh had a dream and told me I had to write my story, so here, I am. I believe dreams do come true, Donagh is amazing.

The rest of 2014 was pretty normal. I had done some healings for clients and loved every bit of it. Donagh had spoken to me about running a meditation group myself. It was something to think about, and the more I thought about it, the more I liked the idea. I decided to give it a go and you know what, I absolutely love it. I am good at it. Even my granddaughter Chloe, loves doing it! Jen even comes to my meditation group every second Friday night. Jen had to laugh as she said "Yeah, I'll give it a go." She didn't know if it would be any good, but she is still coming and loving it.

My own dreams were still full on. Some of my dreams were about my ex-husband, John. I used to wake up frustrated. I wondered why I dreamt of him. But I worked out my dreams were showing me my healing I had done. My ex-husband has stopped controlling my dreams. I was now in control. I didn't feel the anger towards him anymore. I was feeling good and it was time for me to finally move on. I would rather be alone for the right reason, than be with someone for the wrong reason!

We were heading for another Christmas, and I was excited. I was heading to Orange with the family. I was having my first Christmas with my best friend Kathy of twenty two years. We had never got to spend a Christmas together and this was the one. It was excellent. I always have sore jaws from laughing, when we are together. I had Christmas breakfast with Sarina's family and lunch with Kathy's family. It was a wonderful day with beautiful gifts and good company.

During my holidays, we had headed to Bathurst for the day to find some bargains. As we parked to get some lunch, there was an antique shop. Kathy loves browsing in them, so I followed her in and started to look around. As I headed out the back of the shop, there on a shelf, to my surprise, were crystal rocks. The crystal rocks were quite big. I thought I would check it out. I asked the shop assistant about the crystal rocks, on the shelf, out the back. I asked if they were for sale. I kept calm, and didn't want to sound excited. I asked how much they were. The shop assistant said she would check with her husband. She came back and said "Fifty dollars, my love, for the three big ones." "Holly s***" I thought. I told her that I would have another look at them. Two minutes later, I was at the counter paying for it. What a bargain! Remember that saying "Someone else's trash is someone else's treasure."

2015 arrived and I believed it would be a good year. I could feel it. Rabbits seemed to be everywhere I went. I even saw rabbits when we left Orange after Christmas holidays and headed home. The motel we booked into had a paddock full of rabbits next door. When I walked out onto the patio adjoining the motel room, all I could see was rabbits in the paddock. Rabbit means that it is a very creative time. When you see a rabbit, it's important to quickly take advantage of any opportunity that comes your way unexpectedly, and yes we did.

When we came home from Christmas holidays, I caught up with Donna and her family. While Gav and Craig did some work on the hot rods, Donna, Sarina, their children and I went swimming. We had a very nice morning and Donna had asked me about doing some workshops at my house. This was perfect as that would bring more new people into my home and to the healing room. This will work for both of us. Brilliant Idea Donna!!! Our bond just keeps getting stronger and stronger. Donna is amazing doing her Numerology workshops. She really does have a gift at teaching.

I had a beautiful dream about Mum coming to visit me at my new home. I was so excited to show her my new home. We held hands, as we walked around and I told her of all the changes I would do if I owned it. About how I would put a massive healing and meditation room down the back and how busy I would be. Mum put her hand on my shoulder and said "You know what you told me, with the fairies, just believe." She was then gone and I woke up.

My next exciting experience was just recently. I was watching TV one night when I saw my first orb. First I thought it was a reflection of the candles. But I moved and so did it. I took my glasses off and wiped them, and put them back on. The orb was still there just hovering. It was just a bit smaller than a tennis ball. The colour of the orb was a cross between a very light cream and grey. Then it just vanished. I was so excited. I'm like a kid clapping my hands, when I get excited. I questioned myself, was it or wasn't it? But yes, I'm very sure it was.

So many amazing things happen. I just love the spiritual side of life. The things that jump into your head and you think where did that just come from? I also just love the spiritual people you meet and the spiritual things you see. I just love this universe. I just love been grateful all day, every day.

They always say that time
changes things
But you actually have to
change them yourself

Andy Warhol,
The philosophy of Andy Warhol

You could say over the last nine years, I have grown. I have learnt to laugh, cry and heal. Most of all, I have learnt to love myself and trust myself.

If someone had said to me nine years ago, it will take you this amount of time to do all that, I would have said no way. I can't do it, and I don't know if I will cope. Yarhoo!! Yes, I did it.

I'm a better person for having to do that all by myself. The lessons that were thrown at me and guess what, I'm a stronger more loving happier person. But most of all, I love myself, and everything about me. I even love my weird and wonderful side.

I'm a happier person who loves life. I go to bed every night and also on waking every morning, saying something I am grateful for. I am not, who I once was, but who I once was, made me who I am today, and I am truly grateful. That, I am!

I love my family, I love my friends, and I absolutely unconditionally love my Indians and my healing room. I thank God and the Indians every day, for choosing me, to share this gift.

2015 has been a good year for me and who knows what's around the next corner. I believe that there is someone special waiting to share their life with me and you know that saying. One day someone will walk into your life, and make you see, why it never worked out with anyone else. As Mum and I both say 'Just Believe!'

I just want to say thank you, from the bottom of my heart. Thank you to everyone who has been a part of my life journey. I love you all.

Always remember in life

Be Kind
Love Yourself
Love your Life
Treat people the way you wish to be treated
Don't confuse a life lesson for a soul mate
Be grateful everyday
But most of all see and feel with your heart
Just believe, believe, believe!

Let Love In,
Feel with the heart

Surrender to the Indians

Native American Indian Healing

Coming from a place of love and light, Dianne (2CrowsFlying) and High Horse channels the Native American Indians to transcend those who enter the healing room to receive healings through the Native American Indians.

The healing room channels Native American Indian healing energy streams which results in both physical and emotional healing. The healing sessions will provide you with physical, mental, emotional and spiritual balance.

To book a healing session please email
Dianne at 2crowsflying@gmail.com
Like me on Facebook: Surrender to the Indians

Testimonials

I had the most wonderful experience of having a healing with Dianne. I had no great expectations. Just knew I needed some healing. The chanting and drumming during the session is wonderful. It opened up my senses and resonated through my body and reached into my soul. I felt at peace for the first time in a long time. I felt the years of grief that I had carried, lifted from my heart. I do believe that was my first step to finally healing and finding some peace after, some tragic losses in my life… From this healing, I have felt so much better and have been taking care of me. I am so grateful to Dianne and the Indians. This healing has opened up a new path of wellbeing for me. Blessings to Dianne and the Indians. **Glennis Smith**

After a very traumatic experience and major lifestyle change… I was always searching for something… A way to release and feel clear of where I'd been, so I could get back on track with where I had to go. Then I found Dianne. She introduced me to her healing room… And wow… So much has happened since my healing with the Indians. I have had a physical clearing of toxins and my mind feels clearer. I also gave up smoking for the past two weeks… Just did it. No reason, just didn't feel like adding more toxins into my body. All these changed have occurred for the better. I know I will be visiting the Indians again soon. **Julie Noy**

Being welcomed into Dianne's home I felt comfortable and at ease. My mind was open. The experience was calming. After my healing, I felt empowered. After sharing my feelings with Dianne, everything came together for me. Things were making sense in my life. I would highly recommend having a healing with Dianne and the Indians. **Lyn Jamieson**

Printed in the United States
By Bookmasters